TOWARD ONE OREGON

Toward One Oregon

RURAL-URBAN INTERDEPENDENCE
AND THE EVOLUTION OF A STATE

Edited by

Michael Hibbard

Ethan Seltzer

Bruce Weber

Beth Emshoff

Oregon State University Press
Corvallis

The paper in this book meets the guidelines for permanence and durability of the Committee on Production Guidelines for Book Longevity of the Council on Library Resources and the minimum requirements of the American National Standard for Permanence of Paper for Printed Library Materials Z39.48-1984.

Publication of this book was made possible in part by subventions from Oregon State University Extension Service, the Portland State University College of Urban and Public Affairs, and the University of Oregon School of Architecture and Allied Arts. The Oregon State University Press is grateful for this support.

Library of Congress Cataloging-in-Publication Data

Toward one Oregon : rural-urban interdependence and the evolution of a state / edited by Michael Hibbard, Ethan Seltzer, Bruce Weber.
   p. cm.
  Includes bibliographical references and index.
  ISBN 978-0-87071-596-9 (alk. paper)
  1. Rural-urban relations–Oregon. 2. Urbanization–Oregon. 3. Rural development–Oregon. 4. Cities and towns–Oregon. 5. Oregon–Economic conditions.   I. Hibbard, Michael. II. Seltzer, Ethan. III. Weber, Bruce A.
HT384.U52O748 2011
307.09795–dc22

2010053105

Oregon State University Press
121 The Valley Library
Corvallis OR 97331-4501
541-737-3166 • fax 541-737-3170
http://oregonstate.edu/dept/press

Contents

Preface
A New Oregon Trail

In 1842 and 1843, wagon trains began the great migration westward over the Oregon Trail. Two years later the Oregon Territory was created, embracing the area west of the Rockies from the forty-second to the forty-ninth parallels. In 1859 the southwestern portion of the territory was admitted to the Union, and Oregon became a state.

In the one hundred and fifty years that have passed since then, the evolution of Oregon's modern economy has followed a path similar to that in many older states. It is a path that diverged early on into two branches, one for the cities and a separate one for the countryside. This persistent divergence—the so-called rural-urban divide—has shaped Oregon's history down through the years and continues to do so.

This book had its seeds in a comprehensive symposium on rural-urban connections.[1] We, the authors, represent the disciplines of history, urban planning, economics, geography, and political science. The book has been a true labor of love for us. Most of us have researched and written extensively on aspects of the rural-urban divide in Oregon. This book sets out to synthesize our findings and those of our colleagues into a single volume that is accessible to a wide audience: fellow researchers, people in public service, community leaders, business leaders, and other interested lay people.

We were motivated by a conviction that, despite much bemoaning to the contrary, the relationship between Oregon's cities and countryside does not have to be a rivalry or a zero-sum game—in fact, we believe that assumption is no longer serving us. We wanted to look instead for opportunities to create a sturdy rural-urban interdependence.

To be sure, current trends have seen severe erosion in the historical connections between rural, natural resource-based economies and urban centers of technology, creativity, and commerce. But trend is not destiny. *Toward One Oregon* paints a sobering but ultimately positive picture, one that we hope will guide and inform policy decisions that are critical to the future vitality and well-being of Oregon, this place we all call home. We hope this book will provide the starting place for a new Oregon Trail—a trail that can lead us on the path to robust and lasting connections between rural and urban Oregon, and thereby increase social and economic opportunity for all Oregonians.

To our knowledge this is the only book that examines the impacts of a state's rural-urban concerns with a particular focus on economic health and political leadership. Most of the authors are faculty members at universities within the Oregon University System, and the book is an uncommon example of collaboration among public universities, which are charged with the vital mission of public service. Now more than ever, universities must become engaged with decisionmakers on public-policy concerns. We offer *Toward One Oregon* as an invitation for communities and their leaders throughout this state to engage in conversations about our collective future.

Acknowledgments

Financial support for *Toward One Oregon* came from Oregon State University, Portland State University, and the University of Oregon. Scott Reed, OSU's vice provost for Outreach and Engagement, put up a $10,000 challenge grant that was matched by Larry Wallack, dean of the College of Urban and Public Affairs at PSU, and also by the dean of the U of O's School of Architecture and Allied Arts, Francis Bronet, and the U of O's vice president for research, Richard Linton. The Ford Family Foundation provided financial support for the symposium.

The core team of *Toward One Oregon* is composed of colleagues and friends who were determined to make this book a reality. They have stayed the course since their very first meeting at the North Willamette Research and Extension Center in Aurora in the summer of 2006. They are: Bruce Weber, Lyla Houglum, and Beth Emshoff from Oregon State University; Ethan Seltzer, Stephanie Hallock, and Sheila Martin from Portland State University; and Mike Hibbard and Megan Smith from the University of Oregon.

Thanks also to Mary Elizabeth Braun, acquisitions editor for the Oregon State University Press, who encouraged us by believing that this book would be an important contribution to the intellectual, cultural, and social development of Oregon and the West. Our final thanks go to Gail Wells, editor extraordinaire, who worked with us to edit the manuscript and prepare it for publication.

Beth Emshoff
Oregon State University
August 2010

Chapter 1
Toward One Oregon
A Declaration of Interdependence

Ethan Seltzer
Michael Hibbard
Bruce Weber

Every state has a legacy of "truths"—those stories we tell each other to explain why the world is organized the way that it is—and every successive generation has to live with that legacy. At the same time, every state is institutionally and legally bound together within a set of borders that are unlikely to change and a governance structure that changes only slowly and incrementally. When those "truths" conflict with each other, particularly within boundaries that won't change, the conflict often results in difficult, ongoing tensions that become the basis for our politics. Differences in such things as economic base, geography and landscape, settlement patterns, and population density within a state, within *our* state, almost always seem to feed political, social, and cultural divisions.

The way Oregon's boundaries were drawn, it sometimes seems they encourage the notion that there is more to be gained from asserting differences than finding common cause. State boundaries, in fact, are artifacts of old stories, old "truths." The nineteenth-century sketching of the state borders of the western United States from a distance, and in tune with nineteenth-century ideas and methods, exerted a profound effect on our ability to meet the challenges facing our families and communities today.

In Oregon these divisions manifest themselves in pairs of opposing terms like wet and dry, east and west, coastal and inland, red and blue, metropolitan Portland and rural Oregon, among others. These dichotomies speak to a history of contested stories that bedevil and paralyze the state from time to time. One has to look no further than Oregon's struggle to modernize its approach to funding public services, and her seeming inability to do so, to see the shadow of unresolved stories and their conflicts at work.

Modernizing public finance is only one of the tests Oregon faces in the early twenty-first century. The state is confronted with new and looming challenges stemming from the evolving nature of our economy, our natural environment, our relationship to the world, and conditions within our society. We are becoming a different place every day, and our understanding of who and what we are needs to change in response.

Though our presence in Oregon puts us all in a common frame, our differing views of what matters, what needs to happen next and how, pull us in different directions. The diversity of communities and attitudes in Oregon is both a resource and a challenge. We all agree that a healthy economy is important. We all agree that environmental quality is critical. We all agree that it is important for people to have knowledge and skills. But the ways in which those goals are sought vary among communities. We need to strengthen the public discourse so that it recognizes and respects those differences and engenders policies that work in every corner of the state. Our state truly is our home, and through our engagement with one another via this institution we call a "state," we'll determine just how happy a home it really is. This is the way it has always been and, as far as we can see, the way that it will always be.

Oregon's urban-rural divide is one of our longest-lasting divisions and an ongoing challenge to our sense of common cause. It is not unique to Oregon; tensions between city and country have a long history in America and have proven to be persistent here and elsewhere. This is not a division that will be going away any time soon. Art, literature, politics, and social movements have all drawn on competing views of the moral significance of city life versus country life to frame issues and present values and ideas. In the deep background is the vision in western culture of country life as the fundamental source of a society's basic values. Raymond Williams (1973), for example, traces the idealization of the rural all the way back to the Roman republic.

In the United States, the virtue of a rural existence is one of the foundational ideas of Jeffersonian democracy. As the Industrial Revolution transformed the nation between the Civil War and World War I, and as cities became economically, politically, and culturally dominant in the period between World Wars I and II, there was great concern about rural decline. The issue received prominent attention in philosophy (e.g., Josiah Royce), literature (e.g., Hamlin Garland, Helen Hunt Jackson, Booth Tarkington, Zona Gale), and politics (most notably Populism and the Granger movement). It reached its zenith after World War I with the regionalist movement in art, literature, and politics (Dorman 1993).

At the same time, the parallel "revolt from the village" (Hilfer 1969) was at least equally vigorous. The reaction to what Karl Marx, in *The Communist Manifesto*, called the "idiocy of rural life" also had its philosophical (e.g., John Dewey), literary (e.g., Theodore Dreiser, Edgar Lee Masters, Sinclair Lewis), and political (most notably the Progressive movement) manifestations. In this formulation, urban life represented progress, enlightenment, and sophistication—a repudiation of supposedly backward and narrow-minded rural ways.

Despite this history of arguing the virtues of city versus country on moral, political, and even spiritual grounds, urban and rural are fuzzy concepts, not precisely defined. Roughly, urban refers to a metropolitan area: a city, its suburbs, and nearby communities caught up in a metropolitan web of commuting and transactions. Rural designates the area distant from these metropolitan hubs. Geographers refer to the area surrounding the metropolis as "hinterland" or "periphery." It is characterized by a less dense population and infrastructure and by real and perceived remoteness from centers of population stemming from both geographical distance and the difficulty and cost of transportation.

Because they are not precisely defined, such paired concepts as urban-rural and metropolitan area-hinterland are used in a number of ways in this book. Different concepts appear in different chapters, and definitions are not always geographically consistent from one chapter to the next. But whatever terms we use, and wherever we may land in the debate between those who idealize rural life and those who idealize life in the city, one fundamental fact remains: without "city" there is no "country," and without "country" there is no "city." One exists because of the other, and in tight correspondence with the other. Odd as it may seem, there is an unavoidable conceptual if not economic and physical interdependence linking city and country, urban and rural.

The urban-rural relationship can therefore be characterized by both interdependence and tension. Make no mistake: this is a tension born of interdependence, not just difference. With this diversity of views built into the very design of the institution we know as Oregon, our success in the coming decades depends on our ability to make constructive use of that interdependence while finding new means for either accommodating or looking past our differences.

It is with these purposes and in this spirit that this book has been created. As both scholars and residents of the state we choose to live in, study, and serve, we believe Oregon needs to find new ways to make the best of her political and social circumstances. Public finance, climate change, and the demands of globalizing economies and cultures make it imperative that Oregon put aside claims that the urban-rural divide is more real and pressing than these and other challenges. In short, as Oregonians, we need to update our stories to arrive at new "truths" if we are to write the next chapters of our shared history in a constructive, sustainable, and satisfying way.

Fundamentally, we are optimists. We believe there is value in the notion of "One Oregon," and that better understanding of that idea would lead Oregon back to the collaborative pioneering that it is known for. There is promise in the Oregon landscape for urban and rural residents alike, as there always has been. Look to the horizon, and urban and rural vanish as meaningful descriptions of what you see. Continuing to perceive the relationship between them as a zero-sum game, with a winner and a loser in all things, has long outlived its usefulness, if it ever was either descriptive or useful.

This book, then, is the story of our search for the interdependence found at the root of what makes Oregon a state, and for the ways in which the contributions of all of us, urban and rural, east and west, coastal and inland, give us a stake in a common future.

The next chapter sets the stage with a discussion of Oregon's current demographics and economics and alternative ways of thinking about urban and rural. The authors suggest that the people who inhabit these places have similar aspirations for themselves and their families, even though they experience widely diverse living environments, assets, and opportunities. What binds rural and urban Oregonians is a web of economic, environmental, social, and political relationships. Among other things, rural areas provide food, natural resources, energy, and ecosystem services to urban people and places, while urban places provide jobs, markets, specialized services and financial capital, and governmental fiscal resources to rural people and places.

We then move to two historical assessments. The first examines the evolution of Oregon's system of cities from the era of Euro-American settlement to the present. Portland established itself as Oregon's premier city in the 1860s and has maintained that position ever since, although another dozen cities have tried to push it aside. Chapter 3 argues that the changing relationships between Portland and Oregon's other towns and cities can best be understood by setting their development side by side and tracing changes in population, economics, and cultural relations in parallel in the different parts of the state. The second historical assessment is from the perspective of the spatial distribution of political and economic power and influence. The author acknowledges that urban-rural relationships are dynamic, always in the process of readjustment, but his reading of Oregon—as well as world—history maintains that these relationships are still characterized by the urban as more powerful and the rural as less powerful.

The next two chapters provide economic assessments of urban-rural relationships. The first examines how the economic links between the Portland metropolitan area and its periphery changed from 1982 to 2006. During that period, the Portland core grew much faster than the periphery, while the periphery became more self-sufficient, producing specialized services that it had previously imported from the core. In general, trade between core and periphery as a share of each region's economic activity has weakened during the past quarter-century. Yet each economy is still affected by the prosperity of the other.

The second economic analysis examines the sources of revenues and expenditures for state services. Because of the reliance of the state's revenue system on income taxes and because of Portland's more robust economy, the Portland metropolitan area contributes more than its share of state revenue, while receiving less than its share of expenditures for state services. The analysis concludes that both urban and rural areas would benefit from stronger economic conditions and higher incomes in rural Oregon.

We then turn to the political implications of Oregon's urban-rural split. Chapter 7 begins with a discussion of the technology-driven economic changes and increased globalization that in the authors' view are driving continued urbanization and associated demographic and social changes. The discussion draws on surveys and analyses of voting patterns to show that people in urban and rural areas hold considerably different perspectives on society and the role that government ought to play. They conclude that Oregon faces real difficulty in addressing many of the policy issues it faces.

Chapter 8 asserts that attention needs to be paid to the urban-rural economic disconnect, using two key industry clusters to show how urban-rural linkages can be strengthened. Industry clusters that span urban and rural areas represent an important opportunity. Strengthening the connections between urban and rural businesses, between rural businesses and urban consumers, and between rural businesses and urban supporting institutions, can improve profitability in both regions and help bridge the urban-rural divide.

We conclude by drawing together the lessons learned and discussing the prospects for making interdependence a cornerstone for competitiveness and prosperity in the years ahead. We acknowledge that such interdependence will not be easy to achieve. Nevertheless, we find room for hope from our observation that people in every corner of Oregon care deeply about this place where they live. We believe their passion can be harnessed in service to a common good. Oregon has a history of rising to a challenge—a history of gathering together and transcending our differences to confront and solve problems that affect us all. There is no reason we can't do it again.

We offer this book as the beginning of what we hope will be a profound reassessment of what makes Oregon a state. Our aim is to find, explore, and ultimately encourage the ties that bind—or could bind—urban and rural people and places together in a common and more effective future.

Bibliography

Dorman, Robert L. 1993. *Revolt of the Provinces: The Regionalist Movement in America, 1920-1945*. Chapel Hill: University of North Carolina Press.

Hilfer, Anthony. 1969. *The Revolt from the Village, 1915-1930*. Chapel Hill: University of North Carolina Press.

Williams, Raymond. 1973. *The Country and the City*. New York: Oxford University Press.

Chapter 2

A Tale of Two Oregons

Common Aspirations, Different Contexts, and Critical Interdependencies in Urban and Rural Oregon

Sheila Martin[1]
Bruce Weber

Introduction

All Oregonians, regardless of where they live, have the same hopes and aspirations for their communities:

— A strong economy offering rewarding jobs and the opportunity to meet a family's basic needs for food and shelter

— Good health and a healthy environment

— Vibrant communities and neighborhoods

— Strong friendships and families

Notwithstanding these common hopes and concerns, Oregonians live in very heterogeneous environments and each region of Oregon faces different challenges and opportunities. While we often characterize the different parts of our state as either rural or urban, there is neither a typically urban nor a typically rural Oregon. The state offers a mixture of different types of urban places, and there is also enormous diversity in the more sparsely settled areas. Nevertheless, many of the challenges and opportunities facing Oregonians are rooted in the complicated relationship between rural and urban Oregon.

Even the definitions of rural and urban are complex and multidimensional. Three characteristics—size, density, and distance—generally define the differences between rural and urban areas. The size of a place, in terms of both population and land area, is one dimension by which ruralness or urbanness is judged; the others are a related dimension, density, and the distances people must travel in the course of their daily lives. These three characteristics affect how Oregonians experience their daily lives: their job opportunities, the impacts of population, the faces they see in their schools, the characteristics of the land surrounding their communities, and their access to important services.

This chapter sets the stage for a discussion about building a shared future for rural and urban Oregon. We begin with a look at the evolution of the urban and rural areas of Oregon over the past century and a half. After exploring alternative definitions of urban and rural, we review the state's long-term population trends and how the resulting population patterns have created the current rural and urban context. Then we compare and contrast some of the key characteristics of metropolitan and nonmetropolitan areas in Oregon. Finally, we examine some ways in which the urban and rural areas of the state are interdependent and contribute to each other's vitality. These economic, social, and environmental interdependencies provide the basis for moving beyond the "two Oregons" and building a future in which both rural and urban assets are employed for the benefit of all.

Defining Urban and Rural

People often think of urban places as busy, crowded, and noisy, while the word rural evokes a sense of open space, a slower pace, peace and quiet. Economists, demographers, and sociologists have developed a number of different definitions of urban and rural areas.

One of the most common definitions draws a distinction between metropolitan and nonmetropolitan counties. One definition of a metropolitan area is a core urban area with a population of fifty thousand or more and consisting of one or more counties, including the counties containing the urban core, plus any adjacent counties that have a high degree of social and economic integration with the urban core, as measured by commuting patterns (Office of Management and Budget 2000, U.S. Census Bureau).[2] By this definition, anyone who resides in a metropolitan county is considered urban, while everyone else is rural. The metropolitan counties in Oregon are highlighted in figure 1. These counties contain 76 percent of Oregon's population and 18 percent of its land area.

One shortcoming of this definition is that, at least in Oregon, there are many places within metropolitan counties that most people would not think of as urban. For example, Yamhill County is considered part of the Portland metropolitan area because it has strong commuting links to the Portland urban center, yet it includes large, sparsely populated agricultural areas. Similarly, much of Marion and Polk counties would seem to most observers very rural, yet because parts of these counties are within the urban core of Salem, which has a population of more than one hundred and fifty thousand, they are regarded as metropolitan counties.

A second definition of rural and urban Oregon might correspond more closely to traditional notions based on population size and population density. This definition, as developed by the U.S. Census Bureau, regards as urban those places[3] with twenty-five hundred or more people that meet certain density criteria, including a core of at least one thousand people per square mile. Open countryside and places with fewer than twenty-five hundred people are considered rural. This definition can be visualized in figure 1 by considering the geographic distribution of incorporated places; those shown in light gray are urban, while everything else is considered rural. Another visualization is presented in figure 2: the darker patches denote the more heavily populated urban areas, and the lighter places denote sparsely populated rural areas. Under this definition, urban Oregon contains 69 percent of the population and 1 percent of the land.

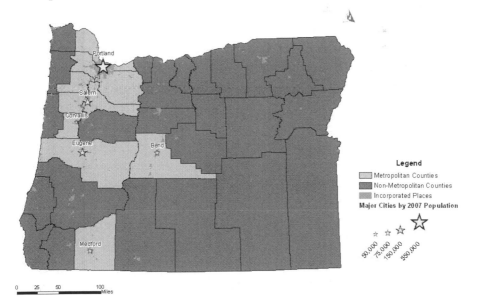

Figure 1. Metropolitan and nonmetropolitan counties and incorporated areas in Oregon. The largest city in each metropolitan area is shown with a star proportional to the city's size. Source: Institute of Portland Metropolitan Studies from U.S. Census Bureau data, http://www.census.gov/population/www/metroareas/metrodef.html.

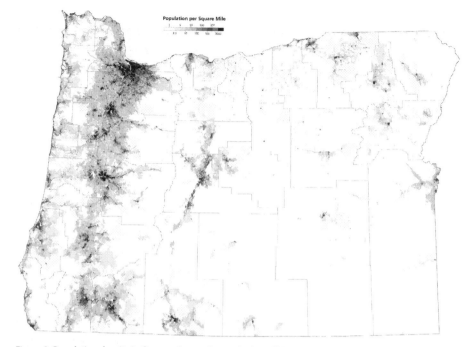

Figure 2. Population density in Oregon. Source: Loy and others 2001, pp. 36-37.

Still another way to think about rural and urban Oregon emphasizes cultural, political, and economic dominance. As mentioned in several chapters of this book, many political scientists and historians discuss urban and rural in terms of the dominance of the urban core over the rural periphery. Economists develop core-periphery models that quantify economic flows of goods, services, and money between an urban core and its rural economic hinterland. In core-periphery models of Oregon, Multnomah County (with Portland as its largest city) constitutes the urban core; the suburban counties of Clackamas and Washington (or all five Oregon counties in the Portland Metropolitan Statistical Area: Clackamas, Columbia, Multnomah, Washington, and Yamhill) are sometimes included in the core. The remainder of the state can be considered the periphery. Some analysts, wishing to define the core's broader functional economic region as its periphery, ignore state lines and draw the Portland core to include Clark County, Washington, and draw the periphery so that it includes counties in southern Washington and/or excludes counties in eastern Oregon.

Many of the statistics presented here are based on the first definition. This is largely a matter of expediency, as many economic and demographic statistics are presented by government agencies in this manner. The prevalence of this definition in the government statistics has, in some ways, shaped our views of the differences between urban and rural areas.

Growth of metro and nonmetro areas in Oregon since 1969

The maps in figure 7 show the changes in the populations of Oregon's counties over time. In 1860, Multnomah County accounted for only about 8 percent of the state's population; more people were living in Marion, Linn, and Lane counties, but by 1880 Multnomah County had 14 percent of the state's population. As farming became more capital- and less labor-intensive, relatively fewer people lived in rural areas, and Multnomah County rose in its dominance, peaking in 1920 with over one-third (35 percent) of the state's population. After that time, the population of the suburban counties, with the assistance of the spread of the automobile, grew as a share of the state's population; the three counties of Multnomah, Clackamas, and Washington have together maintained about 40 percent of the state's population since 1940 (table 1, figure 3), this share remaining relatively steady as the dominance of Multnomah County has fallen relative to that of the suburban counties.

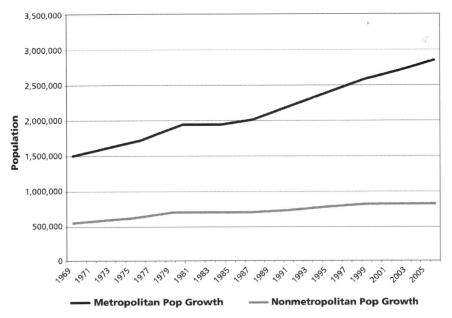

Figure 3. Population growth in metropolitan and nonmetropolitan counties in Oregon, 1969 to 2006. Source: Regional Economic Information System, Bureau of Economic Analysis, U.S. Department of Commerce, Table CA04, http://www.bea.gov/regional/reis/.

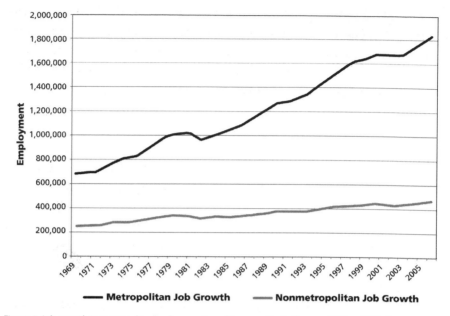

Figure 4. Job growth in metropolitan and nonmetropolitan counties in Oregon, 1969 to 2006. Source: Regional Economic Information System, Bureau of Economic Analysis, U.S. Department of Commerce, Table CA25, http://www.bea.gov/regional/reis/.

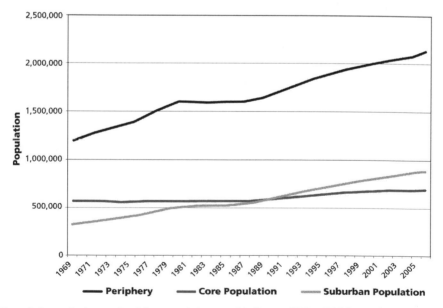

Figure 5. Core, suburban, and periphery population growth in Oregon, 1969 to 2006. Source: Regional Economic Information System, Bureau of Economic Analysis, U.S. Department of Commerce, Table CA04, http://www.bea.gov/regional/reis/.

Under the contemporary definitions, the population of Oregon's metropolitan counties has grown faster than that of nonmetropolitan counties since 1969. During that time, the eleven metropolitan counties roughly tripled in population, while the twenty-five nonmetropolitan counties roughly doubled (figure 3). Since job growth and population growth usually, but not always, coincide, we also observe that job growth has been faster in metropolitan counties (figure 4).

Viewed in terms of the economic dominance of Portland and its suburbs, however, a different picture of population and job growth emerges, revealing the relative stagnation of Multnomah County (which contains the city of Portland proper) and the vitality of the Portland suburbs and the rest of the state. While the population of Multnomah County has grown very modestly, population growth in the two primary Portland suburban counties and in the rest of the state has been significant since 1969 (figure 5). Likewise, job growth has been fastest in the two main suburban counties and the rest of the state, and slowest in the state's largest city (figure 6). Given the relatively slow growth of the nonmetro counties observed in the earlier metro-nonmetro comparison, these figures suggest that population and job growth in Oregon have been concentrated in metropolitan counties other than Multnomah County.

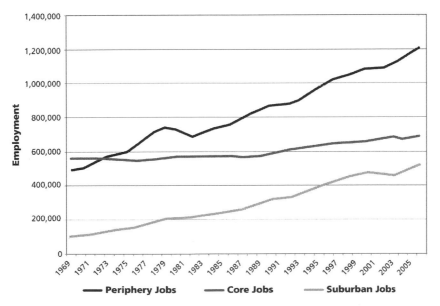

Figure 6. Core, suburban, and periphery job growth in Oregon, 1969 to 2006. Source: Regional Economic Information System, Bureau of Economic Analysis, U.S. Department of Commerce, Table CA25, http://www.bea.gov/regional/reis/.

The emerging dominance of the Portland metropolitan area since 1860

Year	1860	1880	1900	1920	1940	1960	1980	2000
Multnomah	4.2	25	103	276	355	523	563	642
Clackamas	3.5	9.3	20	38	57	113	242	324
Washington	2.8	7.1	15	26	39	92	246	398
Tri-County	10.5	41.4	138	340	451	728	1051	1364
Oregon	52.47	174.77	413.54	783.39	1,089.68	1,768.69	2,633.16	3,421.40
Multnomah, % of state	8.01%	14.30%	24.91%	35.23%	32.58%	29.57%	21.38%	18.76%
Tri-County, % of state	20.01%	23.69%	33.37%	43.40%	41.39%	41.16%	39.91%	39.87%

Table 1. Population and percent of population for Multnomah and its primary suburban counties (thousands). Source: Loy et al. 2001, 27.

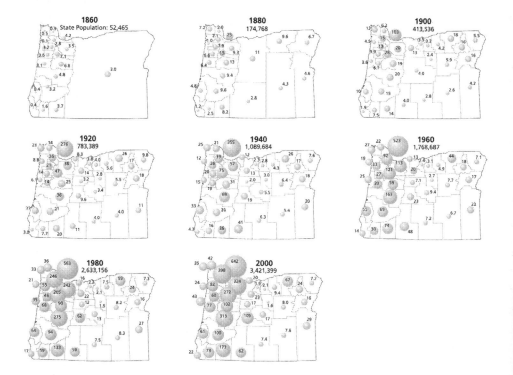

Figure 7. Population in Oregon's counties, 1860 to 2000. On each map, county populations shown on sphere proportional to county population at that date. Source: Loy et al. 2001.

Oregon's Metropolitan and Nonmetropolitan Areas: Current Economic and Social Context

Urban and rural places are shaped by common forces—globalization, federal and state government policy, technological change, and economic and social dynamics in the nation and in neighboring states. These forces work themselves out differently in urban and rural places in part because of differences in size, population density, and distance. In Oregon, as in many other states, their influence is also affected by historical rural-urban differences in settlement patterns, climate, geography, and land ownership. In this section we examine differences in land ownership between urban and rural areas, as well as the economic and demographic outcomes of size, density, and distance; these include the industrial base, income and wages, unemployment and poverty, cost of living, commuting patterns, and ethnic diversity.

Over half (56 percent) of Oregon's land is publicly owned, with the federal government the dominant landowner (figure 8). In metro counties 51 percent of the land is privately owned; in nonmetro counties, 42 percent. Though there is much public land even in metro counties, its impact on local

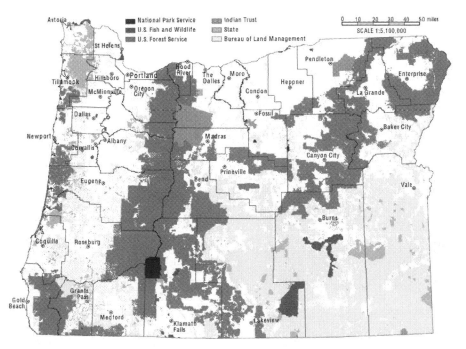

Figure 8. Public land ownership in Oregon. Source: U.S. Department of the Interior, Bureau of Land Management.

government is more significant in rural areas because rural local governments, especially counties, have historically based their budgets on revenue
associated with public lands. When the federal government changes its
revenue-sharing policy, as it did in the recent decision to phase down the Se-
cure Rural Schools revenues associated with federally owned timber, counties
that depend on such revenues are particularly affected—constrained in raising
taxes by limits in the state constitution and often hampered as well by difficult
local economic conditions.

Both metropolitan and nonmetropolitan residents depend on manufacturing and services for jobs. Metropolitan economies are more specialized in
professional services, while nonmetropolitan areas are more specialized in
natural-resource industries and public-sector employment (figure 9). Nevertheless, Oregon's metropolitan counties are among the leading agricultural
counties in the state (figure 10): Marion, Clackamas, and Washington counties were among the state's top five agricultural counties in 2007, generating

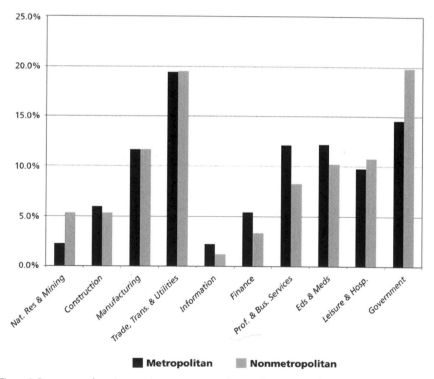

Figure 9. Percentage of employment by sector, metropolitan and monmetropolitan areas, 2007. Source: Oregon
Employment Department, Covered Employment and Wages, 2007 Summary report, http://www.qualityinfo.org/
olmisj/CEP.

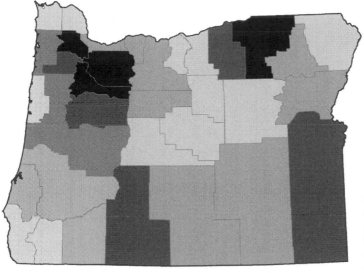

Figure 10. Agricultural sales by county, 2007, in $1,000s. Source: Oregon Department of Agriculture 2007.

Total Sales ($1,000s)

$10,000 - $50,000	$160,000 - $300,000
$50,000 - $80,000	$300,000 - $600,000
$80,000 - $160,000	

more than one-fourth of the state's agricultural sales. However, because they are also influenced by the urban core, they are not nearly as dependent on farm income as are the more rural counties.

Per capita income and average wage per job are higher in metropolitan areas, and wages and incomes have grown faster in metropolitan than in nonmetropolitan areas since 1969 (figure 11, figure 12). In part, this is due to the relatively higher dependence of people in nonmetropolitan areas on fixed sources of income such as Social Security (figure 13). In addition, some of the state's persistently high unemployment rates occur in nonmetropolitan counties, where the closure of one important employer can throw a significant percentage of workers into unemployment (figure 14). Together, lower wages, higher unemployment, and a greater reliance on fixed incomes mean that poverty, although often thought of as an inner-city phenomenon, is a problem also for nonmetropolitan counties (figure 15).

While wages and income are lower in rural areas, the cost of living is often lower as well. Figure 16 shows the amount of income required in 2008 for a family of four (consisting of two adults, one preschooler, and one school-aged child) to adequately meet their basic needs without public or private assistance. This standard considers all basic expenses, including food, housing,

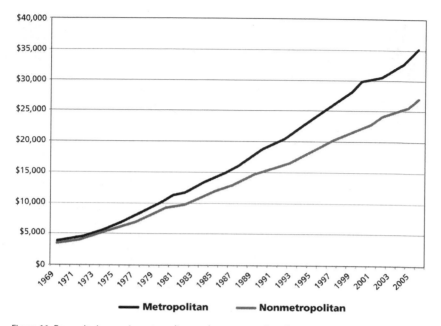

Figure 11. Per capita income in metropolitan and nonmetropolitan Oregon, 1969 to 2006. Source: Regional Economic Information System, Bureau of Economic Analysis, U.S. Department of Commerce, Table CA1-3, http://www.bea.gov/regional/reis/.

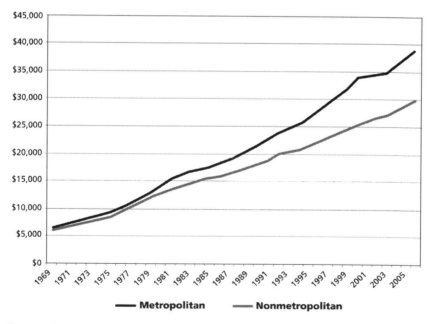

Figure 12. Average annual wage per job in metropolitan and nonmetropolitan Oregon, 1969 to 2006. Source: Regional Economic Information System, Bureau of Economic Analysis, U.S. Department of Commerce, Table CA34, http://www.bea.gov/regional/reis/.

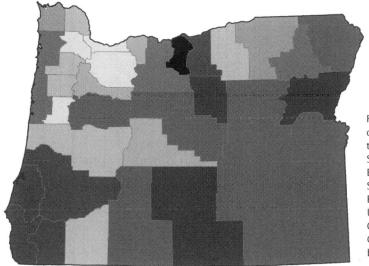

Figure 13. Percentage of income from transfer payments. Source: Regional Economic Information System, Bureau of Economic Analysis, U.S. Department of Commerce, Table CA35, http://www.bea.gov/regional/reis/.

Percent of Income

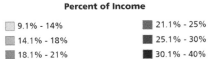

9.1% - 14%	21.1% - 25%
14.1% - 18%	25.1% - 30%
18.1% - 21%	30.1% - 40%

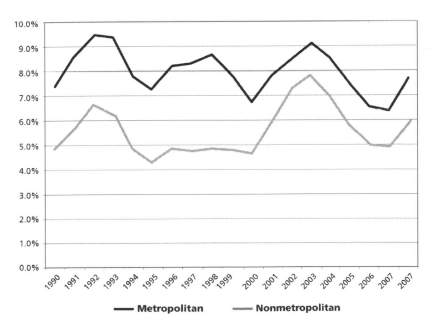

Figure 14. Average annual unemployment rates in metropolitan and nonmetropolitan Oregon, 1990-2008 (figures not seasonally adjusted). Source: Oregon Employment Department, Local Area Employment Statistics, http://www.qualityinfo.org/olmisj/labforce.

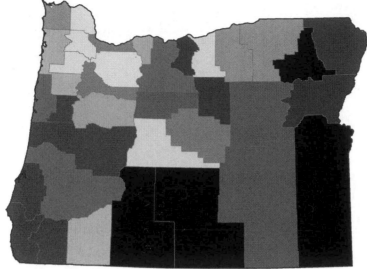

Figure 15. Percentage
of households in
poverty, 2000. Source:
U.S. Census Bureau,
Census 2000 Summary
File 3. http://www.
census.gov/main/
www/cen2000.html.

6.1% - 10%	12.1% - 13%
10.1% - 11%	13.1% - 15%
11.1% - 12%	15.1% - 16%

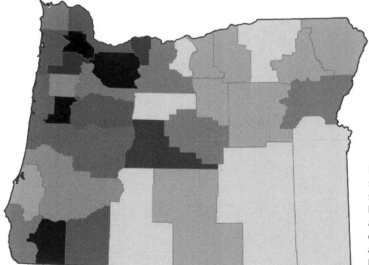

Figure 16. Self-
sufficiency income
standard in 2008 for a
household with two
adults, one preschool
child, and one school-
aged child. Source:
Pearce 2008.

$34,000 - $35,500	$38,500 - $42,500
$35,000 - $36,500	$42,500 - $50,000
$36,500 - $38,500	$50,000 - $60,500

transportation, health care, child care, and taxes (Pearce 2008). Figure 16 shows that the most expensive places to live on the average are indeed the metropolitan counties; however, there is variation within each category.

Density and distance both cause commuters to spend time in their cars (figure 17). For urban commuters, the reason may be getting stalled in traffic; for some rural commuters it is because of the longer distances they must travel. The shortest average commute times are in remote rural counties where commuting to another community is not feasible.

We often think of cities as being the most racially and ethnically diverse places in our state, while our images of rural areas are of ethnically homogenous places that have changed little since settlement. But today, racial and ethnic diversity is increasing in both metropolitan and nonmetropolitan Oregon, although in different ways. Metropolitan Oregon has a higher concentration of African Americans and Asians, while nonmetropolitan counties have higher concentrations of Latinos and Native Americans (figure 18). Oregon restricted post-Civil War African American immigration, and until World War II there was very little racial diversity in the state. Oregon had a population of fewer than

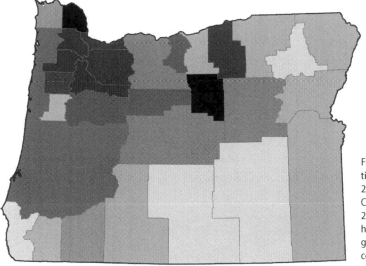

Figure 17. Mean travel time to work (minutes), 2000. Source: U.S. Census Bureau, Census 2000 Summary File 3, http://www.census. gov/main/www/ cen2000.html.

Minutes

14.4 - 16.3	19.6 - 22.2
16.4 - 18.1	22.3 - 26.2
18.2 - 19.5	26.3 - 30.8

Figure 18. Percentage of white, non-Hispanic residents in Oregon, 2000. Source: U.S. Census Bureau, Census 2000 Summary File 1, http://www.census.gov/main/www/cen2000.html.

▨ 64.1% - 78%	▓ 91.1% - 94%
▨ 78.1% - 87%	■ 94.1% - 96%
▓ 87.1% - 91%	

eighteen hundred African Americans in 1940. African Americans migrated to the area during World War II to work at the shipyards in Portland and Vancouver. By 1946 more than fifteen thousand African Americans lived in the Portland area, many in Vanport, the city constructed to house shipyard workers and their families. As white families left Vanport after the war, the concentration of African Americans increased, and Vanport became a relatively concentrated black community (Maben 1987, 86) until it was destroyed by a flash flood in 1948. After the flood, the African American community resettled mostly in northeast Portland. Today, Portland's population includes about thirty-five thousand African Americans, representing 6.6 percent of the city's population and more than half of the state's sixty-three thousand African American citizens.

Interdependence of Rural and Urban Oregon

Dabson (2007) summarizes rural contributions to metropolitan prosperity and urban contributions to rural prosperity in America:

> America's rural and urban areas share many degrees of interdependence; rural areas provide critical consumption goods for

metropolitan consumers, such as food, energy, lower-cost land and labor, and unique experiences; metro areas constitute the end market for rural production; provide specialized services; offer diverse job opportunities; and generate resources for public and private investment in rural America. (2)

To some degree, this is certainly true in Oregon. Although urban and rural areas of Oregon face different challenges and opportunities, they are interdependent through their exchange of goods and services (both material and environmental), people, and taxes and public expenditures. Urban areas, with higher incomes, are able to provide a more-than-proportionate share of Oregon's specialized services such as health care and financial and business services, as well as public funding for schools, infrastructure, and other programs. Rural areas, with more natural resources, provide a more-than-proportionate share of energy and environmental goods and services.

An important source of interdependence is that people move between urban and rural areas, bringing with them the values and norms from their place of origin and gaining an understanding of life and challenges in new surroundings. Young people often move from rural to urban areas to get additional education and higher-paying jobs. And many commuters travel to work from rural to urban areas. These trends indicate that Dabson (2007) is correct in his characterization of rural areas as providing workforce to urban industry. In addition, older adults often move from urban to rural areas to retire and enjoy amenities and lower living costs.

Market-driven trade in goods and services

Trade in goods and services between rural and urban areas, both within industry clusters and between industries and consumers, is another key source of interdependence. The Portland core (Multnomah, Washington, and Clackamas counties) exports 37 percent of its production outside the state and 4 percent to its trade-area periphery of western and central Oregon. The periphery is somewhat more self-contained, exporting 33 percent of its production outside the state and 2 percent to the core (see Chapter 5). These percentages indicate that, although the overall volume of trade is significant, the interdependence between core and periphery is not as strong as one might think; a global economy and lower transportation costs have made distance less important to trade than it once was. However, for some critical goods and services, interdependence is very real. These goods include livestock, crops, seafood, and manufactured goods such as processed food and wood products. Important services include cultural, hospitality, and recreational services, medical services, energy, higher education, and environmental services.

To further illustrate Oregon's urban-rural interdependencies, we examine the last four of these services: urban areas are the primary suppliers of medical services and higher education, and rural areas are the primary suppliers of electric power and environmental goods and services.

In order to take advantage of economies of scale, medical care is increasingly centralized in urban hubs. As a result, access to health care is generally less available in rural areas. Much of rural Oregon has been designated as "medically underserved" (figure 19), based on low numbers of primary-care physicians and measures of infant mortality, poverty, and high proportions of elderly people. Access to hospitals is also a concern in rural areas. The mean travel time to hospitals in Oregon is 23.7 minutes, but for many it is much longer. In some remote areas it takes more than an hour to reach the nearest hospital (figure 20). However, there are medically underserved areas

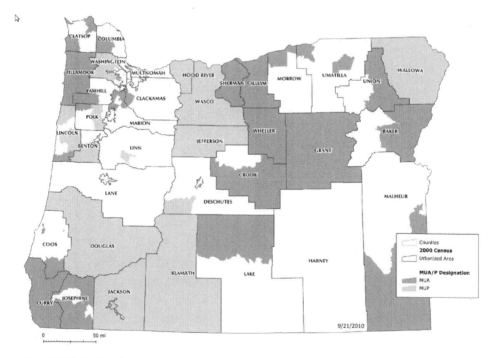

Figure 19. Medically underserved areas (dark gray) and populations (light gray) in Oregon, 2007. Source: Oregon Department of Human Services.

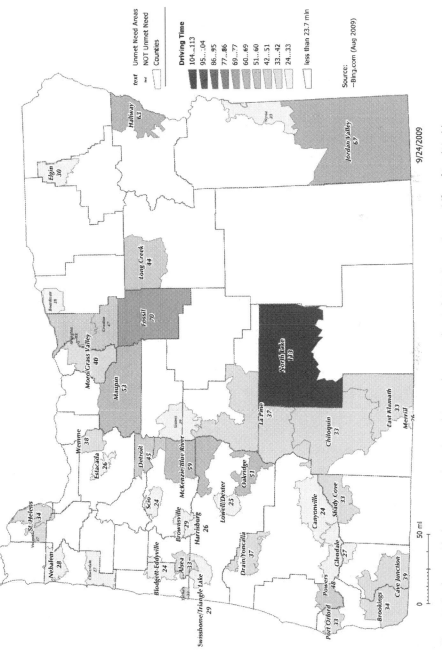

Figure 20. Rural areas with above-average (mean) travel time to the nearest hospital, 2009. Source: Oregon Office of Rural Health.

and populations (groups that face economic, cultural, or linguistic barriers to health care) in both urban and rural areas.[4]

Six of the eight Oregon University System higher-education institutions are in metropolitan counties, and in the fall of 2008 only about 9 percent of total enrollment in OUS institutions was in the two nonmetro universities (Oregon University System Fact Book 2008). Since about 24 percent of the population resides in nonmetro counties, rural high school graduates wishing to attend public universities in Oregon will likely end up in a metropolitan county. Access to community colleges, where many students enroll for the first two years of college courses, is more widespread: ten of the seventeen community colleges in the state have central campuses in nonmetropolitan counties.

Most of the electric power generation capacity in Oregon is in nonmetropolitan areas (figure 21). Rural areas not only provide relatively cheap and abundant hydropower but also offer opportunities for increasing the supply of solar and wind power, as well as fulfilling the emerging promise of wave-

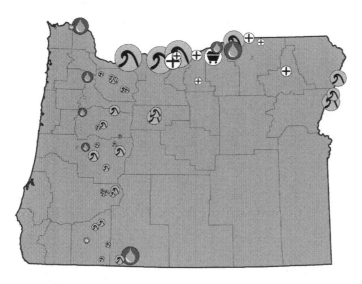

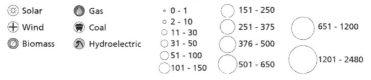

Figure 21. Power generation facilities and capacity in Oregon. Sources: U.S. Energy Information Administration, State Energy Profiles: Oregon, http://tonto.eia.doe.gov/state/state_energy_profiles. cfm?sid=OR#Datum; Loy et al. 2001.

generated power. The mostly urban universities have the capacity to develop technology for realizing the potential of these new energy sources. This presents an opportunity for rural and urban Oregon to work together to capture a position of leadership in the next generation of sustainable energy.

Rural areas also provide natural resources and environmental goods and services that serve the needs of the entire state. Much of the habitat for animals and plants that populate the region is in rural areas. The clean water and clean air available to both urban and rural residents depend on the resources in rural areas: pure water, fish habitat in streams cooled by trees, living plants that sequester carbon. There are large areas in rural Oregon where the cost of carbon sequestration is very low. Hence these areas furnish a valuable ecosystem service, that of absorbing carbon dioxide from the air for the benefit of the population as a whole.

Public-sector taxes and spending

The revenue-sharing system in Oregon creates a financial interdependence among metropolitan and nonmetropolitan areas. Cortright (2008) has estimated that metro Portland provides $550 million more annually in state taxes and fees than it receives in state services and shared revenues. This net outflow is mostly spent on education and health programs in the rest of Oregon (see Chapter 6). As a result, the health of public services in Oregon depends heavily on the health of the Portland economy. The system ensures that if the metropolitan area's economy is weak, nonmetropolitan areas will suffer as well, and when rural areas are thriving, fewer resources are needed to equalize opportunity for rural and urban residents.

Two-thirds of the state's general-fund budget is spent on education. The K-12 system of elementary and secondary schools accounts for 43 percent of total state spending. Operating expenditures per student are much higher in rural areas, in part because of transportation costs and higher ratios of teachers to students; small classes are difficult to avoid in areas where critical mass simply cannot be achieved (figure 22). Even with funding formulas that generate higher state aid to schools in rural areas, many rural schools had in 2005 cut the school week to four days—a solution that at that time seemed unfathomable in urban areas (figure 23). Despite the challenges facing rural schools and the perception that education in rural areas is substandard, student performance is often high. Excellent schools exist in both rural and urban areas, as do schools that do not meet state reading standards (figure 24).

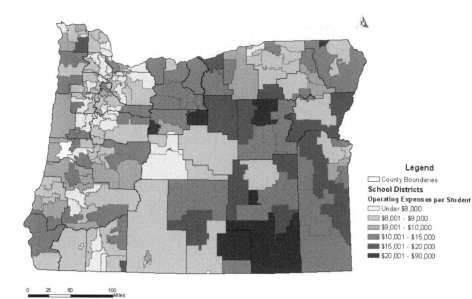

Figure 22. Operating expenditures per student in Oregon school districts, 2006-2007. Source: Oregon Department of Education, http://www.ode.state.or.us/sfda/reports/r0091Select.asp.

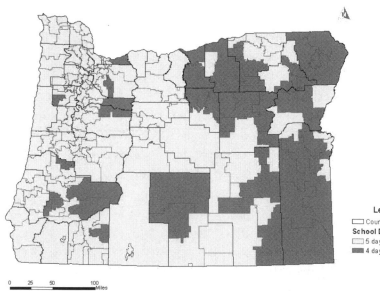

Figure 23. Oregon school districts operating on four-day weeks, 2005. Source: Oregon Department of Education, http://www.ode.state.or.us/.

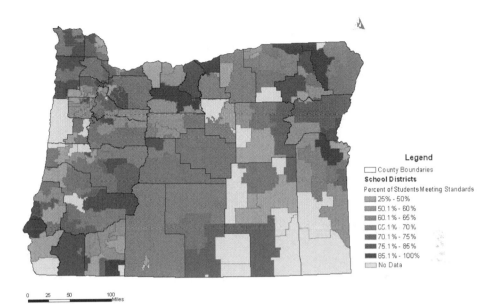

Figure 24. Percentage of eighth-grade students meeting or exceeding state reading standards, 2007-2008.
Source: Oregon Department of Education, http://www.ode.state.or.us/.

A Shared Future

All Oregonians face challenges, but many of them manifest themselves differently in urban and rural areas: the struggle to fund quality education, the need to create an economy that offers opportunities for a decent standard of living, access to and ability to pay for quality health care, and a healthy social and physical environment. Despite the differences in how we experience, face, and meet these challenges, our fates are intertwined.

Bibliography

Cortright, Joe. 2008. *Fiscal flow analysis*. Portland OR: Impresa Inc. http://www.impresaconsulting.com/.

Dabson, Brian. 2007. "Rural-urban interdependence: Why metropolitan and rural America need each other." Background paper prepared for the Blueprint for American Prosperity, November 2007. The Brookings Institution, Washington, D.C. http://www.brookings.edu/projects/blueprint/whatis; scroll down to "additional resources." Consulted June 4, 2009.

Isserman, Andrew. 2005. In the national interest: Defining rural and urban correctly in research and public policy. *International Regional Science Review* 28(4): 465-99.

Loy, William G., Stuart Allan, Aileen Buckley, and Jim Meacham. 2001. *Atlas of Oregon.* Eugene: University of Oregon Press.

Maben, Manley. 1987. *Vanport.* Portland: Oregon Historical Society Press.

National Energy Technology Laboratory. 2007. *Carbon Sequestration Atlas of the United States and Canada.* U.S. Department of Energy, Office of Fossil Energy.

Office of Management and Budget. 2000. Standards for Defining Metropolitan and Micropolitan Statistical Areas. Notice. *Federal Register* 65: 82228-38.

Oregon Department of Agriculture. 2007. *Oregon Agripedia.* Salem, OR.

Oregon Office of Rural Health. http://www.ohsu.edu/xd/outreach/oregon-rural-health/data/publications/maps.cfm.

Oregon University System. 2008. Fact Book. http://www.ous.edu/factreport/factbook/.

Pearce, Diana M. 2008. *The Self-Sufficiency Standard for Oregon 2008.* Report prepared for WorkSystem, Inc. http://www.selfsufficiencystandard.org/pubs.html.

U.S. Census Bureau. *Metropolitan and Micropolitan Statistical Areas.* http://www.census.gov/population/www/metroareas/metroarea.html. Accessed January 8, 2009.

Chapter 3
From Urban Frontier to Metropolitan Region
Oregon's Cities from 1870 to 2009

Carl Abbott

This is an investigation of the evolution of Oregon's system of cities from the era of settlement to the present. We can best understand the changing relationships between Portland and Oregon's other towns and cities if we set their development side by side, tracing changes in population, economics, and cultural relations in parallel in the different parts of the state. In the process I use some of the theoretical models of urban geography to inform the historical analysis. In particular, it is useful to examine the relative sizes of Oregon cities over time and to evaluate the extent to which Portland has functioned as what geographers call a "primate city," one that far outstrips its potential rivals and competitors in a region or nation. In some cases a primate city may be a political and economic capital that has overwhelmed provincial rivals, as with Paris, Buenos Aires, and Bangkok. In other cases it emerged as the center through which European imperial powers deliberately dominated colonial possessions, concentrating governmental authority and commerce in places like Accra, Jakarta, Abidjan, and Luanda, while leaving secondary cities far behind.

The discussion divides the state's history into three roughly equal periods. The first starts in the 1870s, when Portland had clearly won out over its close-in neighbors and the first railroad construction began to give Oregon its modern economic geography, and runs to 1920. The second covers the period from 1920 to 1970, when Oregon had a relatively stable economy based on the production and processing of natural resources. The third begins with the political and economic transformations of the 1970s and covers the years to the present.

Portland Ascendant, 1870-1920

The greater Northwest was the nation's hot corner at the end of the nine-teenth century and the beginning of the twentieth. From St. Paul and Omaha to Denver and Butte and on to Portland and Seattle, the northwest quadrant of the U.S. attracted the attention of investors, travelers, and journalists. In the decades before World War I, Bostonians and Londoners who came looking for western cities usually covered territory bracketed by Minneapolis, Denver, San Francisco, and Seattle, with stops perhaps in Salt Lake City, Portland, Spokane, Helena, and Bismarck. That's the area where William Thayer found *Marvels of the New West* in 1887, where Julian Ralph explored *Our Great West* in 1893, and where Edward Hungerford found candidates to profile in *The Personality of American Cities* in 1913. It's the same territory that the distin-guished English observer James Bryce traversed to research his chapter on "The Temper of the West" in *The American Commonwealth*, published in 1888, and that Rudyard Kipling reported on in *From Sea to Sea* (1899), with chapters on San Francisco, Portland, Seattle, Salt Lake City, and Omaha. In 1914, the sober officials who organized the Federal Reserve Bank were "impressed with the growth and development of the States of Idaho, Washington, and Oregon . . . with continued growth of that region it is reasonable to expect that in a few years the capital and surplus of its member banks will be suffi-cient to justify the creation of an additional Federal Reserve district" (Reserve Bank Organization Committee 1914).

Portland grew up with this vast region. It started the 1870s as the leading city in Oregon and the larger Columbia Basin. It had occupied a strategic location for tapping the trade of the Willamette Valley and the Columbia River and had consolidated that lead with a series of incremental victories over potential rivals such as Milwaukie, Oregon City, and St. Helens. Portland entrepreneurs dominated Columbia River shipping and controlled the tele-graph line and railroads that pushed southward toward California in the 1870s and 1880s. The arrival of transcontinental rail connections after 1883 and the branch lines that helped to open up the vast interior of the Columbia Basin cemented the city's position. The city's bankers financed the growing trade in natural resources and Portland merchants supplied the needs of small-town consumers. The sense of connection shows in a special issue of *The Oregonian* from January 1, 1910: the city newspaper identified the progress of the entire Columbia Basin as its own with a series of headlined stories: INTERIOR TOWNS FACE BRIGHT FUTURE. RAILROADS WILL PIERCE GREAT TIMBER BELT. WHEAT OUTPUT

WILL BE ENORMOUS. DESCHUTES KNOWN AS RIVER OF GOLD. OREGON FORGING TO
THE FRONT AS LIVESTOCK STATE.

Even as loggers pushed into the Cascades and Coast Range and farmers
cultivated millions of acres of new fields and orchards, Portland reached its
greatest dominance over competing cities. Observers agreed that Tacoma
might be a manufacturing center and Seattle a fast-growing port, but Portland was "a blend of these two, with the added characteristic of the central
market town for a region of intensive agricultural development" ("The future
of north coast cities" 1909; Croly 1912). Data on Oregon's urban system con-
firm that Portland was a primate city relative to its rivals in Oregon and the
Pacific Northwest.

One way to measure Portland's primacy is by its share of total state
population, which grew very rapidly from 9 percent in 1870 to 20 percent in
1890, edged higher to 22 percent in 1900, and shot upward again in the early
twentieth century to a maximum of 33 percent in 1920 (table 1). Despite the
headlong development of Oregon's agricultural, ranching, and timber counties during this period, Portland grew even more rapidly.

We can also measure Portland's population against that of other Oregon
towns and cities. In large, historically mature, and regionally complex nations, such as present-day Germany, China, and the United States, urban
systems often follow a rank-size pattern in which the second-largest city contains roughly half the population of the largest, the third city is one-third the
size of the largest, and so on, through populations of one-fourth, one-fifth,
one-sixth, one-seventh, and further down. In contrast, early Oregon showed
a distinctly unbalanced pattern. The second-largest city in 1880, Astoria,
was only one-seventh as large as Portland, and Salem, the third-largest city,
was one-eighth as large. Four decades later, the imbalance was even deeper.
Salem was only one-sixteenth the size of Portland, Astoria one-eighteenth,

1880		1900		1920	
Portland + East Portland	20,511	Portland	90,426	Portland	258,280
Astoria	2,803	Astoria	8,381	Salem	17,679
Salem	2,538	Baker City	6,163	Astoria	14,027
The Dalles	2,232	Pendleton	4,406	Eugene	10,593
Albany	1,867	Salem	4,258	Baker City	7,729

Table 1. Largest Oregon cities in 1880, 1900, and 1920. Source: Loy et al. 2001.

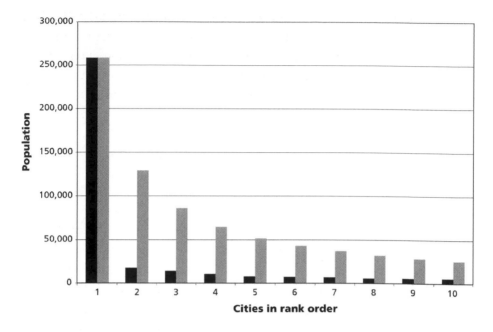

Figure 1. Oregon cities 1920: rank-size model (see table 2) and actual populations. The bars represent (from left to right) Portland, Salem, Astoria, Eugene, Baker, Pendleton, La Grande, The Dalles, Medford, and Corvallis.

Eugene one-twenty-fourth, and Baker City one-thirty-third. Looking at city population figures in the aggregate, Portland in 1880 was larger than the sixteen next-larger towns added together, and it was more than *twice* as large as the four next-larger towns added together. The advantage increased for the next forty years. Portland was twice as large as the next ten towns in 1890, the next thirteen in 1900, the next eighteen in 1910, and the next *twenty* in 1920 (figure 1, table 2).

These data make clear the degree to which Portland had effectively separated itself from half a dozen potential rivals located across the northern half of the state. From the 1870s through the early 1900s Oregon had plenty of other cities with big ambitions—Astoria, Albany, Salem, The Dalles, Pendleton, and Baker City—but each had handicaps in competing with Portland (table 2).

Astoria was the second-largest city in Oregon in 1880 and 1900, but then it began a slow, steady descent in relative size. Its problem then as now was a geographically constrained hinterland that was limited to timber and fish harvesting, resources that were and are vulnerable to over-harvesting. As a port, Astoria ironically suffered from being too close to the ocean. It is almost always cheaper to transport heavy cargoes by water than by land. Portland won its early rivalries because it was the effective head of navigation on the Willamette, and its business interests worked assiduously to maintain a usable harbor and channel to the Pacific, lobbying the federal government and creating the Port of Portland for this purpose in 1891. With railroads also converging on Portland, Astoria remained a minor port at the end of the rail line.

	1870	1880	1890	1900	1910	1920	1930
Portland	1	1	1	1	1	1	1
Salem	2	3	3	5	2	2	2
Oregon City	3	6	5	7	13	11	13
The Dalles	4	4	6	6	8	8	12
Jacksonville	5	11	22				
Eugene	6	9	10	8	4	4	3
Astoria	7	2	2	2	3	3	6
Baker City	8	7	7	3	6	5	9
Albany		5	4	9	14	13	14
Pendleton		13	9	4	12	6	11
Klamath Falls					17	14	4
Medford			17	15	5	9	5
Corvallis		8	12	14	11	10	10
Bend						12	7
	1940	1950	1960	1970	1980	1990	2000
Portland	1	1	1	1	1	1	1
Salem	2	2	3	3	3	3	2
Oregon City	13	*	*	*	*	*	*
The Dalles	12	17	12	14	15	14	16
Jacksonville							
Eugene	3	3	2	2	2	2	3
Astoria	6	7	11	15	17	16	14
Baker City	6	12	15	17	19	21	
Albany							
Pendleton	9	8	8	11	12	11	8
Klamath Falls	4	6	7	7	8	8	11
Medford	5	4	4	5	4	4	4
Corvallis	10	5	5	4	5	5	9
Bend	7	9	10	9	7	7	5

Table 2. Oregon cities ranked by population. Notes: Metropolitan and micropolitan area populations are used for recent decades when designated by the U.S. Census. The table includes every Oregon city that ranked in the top five in any one of the fourteen census years, and it shows rankings from 1 through 25. Oregon City included with Portland metropolitan area population since 1950. Sources: Loy et al. 2001; U.S. Census Bureau.

The Dalles, the state's fourth-largest city in 1880, also dropped steadily in rank thereafter. It had the opposite problem from that of Astoria, lying not too close to the ocean but too far away. The Columbia River rapids had been a great commercial emporium for native peoples, where coastal traders could exchange fish and cedar products for meat and hides gathered by interior tribes. In the mid-nineteenth century, however, the sets of rapids that bracketed The Dalles to the east and west required portage railroads and expensive canal/lock systems that were not completed until 1896 at the Cascades and 1915 at Celilo Falls. Railroads up the Deschutes River were also not completed until construction of competing lines by the Harriman and Hill interests in the early twentieth century.

Albany and Salem (and McMinnville, Monmouth, Corvallis, Harrisburg, and Eugene) were boxed in by Portland. When early railroad builders logically preferred routing their lines over the easy grade of the Columbia River Gorge to attempting expensive routes over Santiam Pass or Willamette Pass, these other Willamette Valley communities had little option but to trade through Portland. With the state capital and associated institutions, Salem maintained second or third rank, but never broke through to rival Portland (as a comparison, consider the way that Columbus, Ohio, has slowly caught up with Cincinnati). Albany's high point was a rank of fourth in 1890, but it had slipped to thirteenth place by 1920.

Farther east, geography also conspired against the emergence of a substantial rival. Pendleton, La Grande, and Baker City each was located in its own small valley, as was Walla Walla across the Washington state line. The result was a series of small cities, each the metropolis of one or two counties, rather than one larger center. Pendleton made a run from thirteenth to fourth place from 1880 to 1900 before dropping back. Baker City burst impressively to third in 1900, but its growth also plateaued in the twentieth century and it fell back in rank. By contrast, Boise is the economic center for the Snake River Plain with a string of secondary cities from Twin Falls to Nampa. Another contrast is the situation of Spokane, which developed as a railroad center and hub of an "inland empire" that took in parts of three states and a Canadian province. There was always much hot air in the idea of an inland empire, but the fact remained that convergent geography made Spokane one of four key rail nodes in the interior West, along with Denver, Salt Lake City, and El Paso.

Data gathered as the basis for designating cities for Federal Reserve Banks in 1914 show Portland's dominance. The federal government asked the nation's

	Oregon	Idaho	Washington	California
Portland	**56**	**10**	**9**	–
	11	16	22.5	9
San Francisco	**16**	**8**	**8**	**208**
	45	12	17	25
Seattle	–	–	**40**	–
	8	–	0.5	1
Spokane	**1**	–	**16**	–
	2	9	5	–
Salt Lake City	–	**12**	–	–
	–	2	2	–
Los Angeles	–	–	–	**24**
	–	–	–	81
Other	–	**6**		**3**
	2	15	8	18

Table 3. Preferences for Federal Reserve city by Pacific and Northwest banks. Note: First-place votes in bold.
Source: Reserve Bank Organization Committee, *Location of Reserve Districts in the United States.*

banks to list first, second, and third choices for a Federal Reserve Bank. Table 3 shows the cities that received first- and second-place votes from Oregon and neighboring states. Among Northwest cities, Portland received seventy-five first-place votes, Seattle forty, and Spokane thirty. For comparison, Denver received 136 votes from Rocky Mountain states, and San Francisco 259. (Denver eventually lost the Federal Reserve Bank to Kansas City, but San Francisco's choice for the West Coast branch was never in serious doubt.) A breakout by state shows that Portland received fifty-six first-place votes from Oregon, with sixteen Oregon banks preferring San Francisco. Portland received the first-place nod from ten of Idaho's forty-five banks (which also split very evenly among Spokane, Salt Lake City, and San Francisco). Portland was the first choice of nine Washington banks, the second choice of twenty-two, and the third choice of fifteen.

The implications are clear. Portland by the early 1910s may have slipped behind Seattle in population because of that city's Klondike gold-rush boom, but it had a much wider commercial and financial reach as the center for most of Oregon, for southwestern Idaho, and for Washington communities along the lower Columbia.[1] It is likely that Oregon's sixteen first-place votes for San Francisco came from the south coast and perhaps the Klamath Basin, where transportation connections to California were strong (although the votes could also have come from bankers who simply saw San Francisco as a city with greater banking resources). The fact that Portland received nine second-place votes from California banks compared to one vote for Seattle also shows the relative prominence of the two Pacific Northwest ports. This analysis matches other efforts to map metropolitan hinterlands in the early twentieth century, such as Roderick McKenzie's mapping of newspaper circulation as a measure of metropolitan influence, which shows *The Oregonian* and the *Oregon Journal* as dominant papers in Oregon, southwestern Washington, and southwestern Idaho in the early 1900s (McKenzie 1933).

Oregon in Balance, 1920-1970

During the middle decades of the twentieth century, the growth of secondary cities gradually reduced the imbalance between Portland and the rest of the state without changing Portland's economic primacy. This era saw the most rapid urban growth in southern-tier cities such as Medford and Klamath Falls, in part the result of new agricultural development with increased investment in irrigation (table 4). Medford moved from seventeenth in 1890 to fifth place among Oregon cities in 1930 and 1940 (see table 2). Klamath Falls also benefited from the construction of a north-south rail line east of the Cascades and the Eugene-Chemult connector over Willamette Pass; it shot from seventeenth place in 1910 to fourth in 1930 and 1940. Again, however, the fragmented geography of the southern Oregon landscape led to the development of a set of small cities rather than one large city. Roseburg, Grants Pass, Medford, and Klamath Falls each developed in its own valley, which meant that there was no southern Oregon city equivalent to Bakersfield, Fresno, or Sacramento.

The share of state population within the city of Portland itself slowly declined from 33 percent in 1920 to 28 percent in 1940, and then more rapidly to 18 percent in 1970. It is more appropriate, however, to use data on

1920		1940		1960	
Portland	258,280	Portland	305,294	Portland metro: three OR counties	728,088
Salem	17,679	Salem	30,908	Eugene metro	162,890
Astoria	14,027	Eugene	20,838	Salem	49,142
Eugene	10,593	Klamath Falls	16,497	Medford	24,425
Baker City	7,729	Medford	11,281	Corvallis	20,669

Table 4. Largest Oregon cities in 1920, 1940, and 1960. Sources: Loy et al. 2001; U.S. Census Bureau.

metropolitan population. Portland was defined by the U.S. Census Bureau as a metropolitan district in 1920 and 1930 and as a three-county metropolitan area in 1940-1970. By this measure, the population of the Portland area was quite stable, at 38 percent of the state population in the 1920 metropolitan district, and 41-42 percent for the three-county metropolitan area for 1950-1970. By the alternative measure of primacy based on the rank-size curve, Portland was larger than the next twenty cities in 1920, but larger than only the next thirteen by 1940, and larger than the next twelve by 1960. It was still overwhelmingly large, but other places were beginning to catch up.

Oregonians during this period continued to understand their state in terms of reciprocal relations between resource-producing regions and Portland as a shipping and processing center. Paved highways for the automobile age also extended outward from Portland and other Willamette Valley cities.[2] For one example, Portland entrepreneurs and engineers were chiefly responsible for building a seventy-mile highway through the Columbia River Gorge in the 1910s, letting adventuresome auto drivers parallel the route of the Union Pacific Railroad past deep chasms and plunging waterfalls to roadhouses and hotels built with Portland money. Portland investors helped Hood River County finance the eastern section of the road to link the county's new orchards to metropolitan and national markets.

Portland industry remained heavily dependent on processing regional raw materials. Solidifying the foundation for continued resource-based industry, shipyards in World War I had employed twelve thousand workers building steel-hulled ships and seventeen thousand workers building wooden-hulled cargo carriers. The largest yard was the Grant-Smith-Porter yard at the foot of Baltimore Street in Portland's St. Johns neighborhood, which employed six thousand workers. Grant-Smith-Porter was one of nearly a score of shipyards that specialized in wooden vessels. They bought their material from booming Portland sawmills and drew workers from the large pool of men with woodworking skills (Sensenisch 1918; *The Oregonian* 1919 and 1920). In 1929, the largest industrial employers were Libby, McNeill, & Libby, Swift & Co., Jantzen Knitting Mills, and Doernbecher Furniture—all companies that turned the products of Oregon's fields and forests into consumer goods (Day and Zimmerman, Inc. 1930, 136-45).

The early twentieth century was a time when Oregonians shared common social ties as well as common economic connections. Class interests and class culture spanned the different corners of the state, dividing communities internally but simultaneously shaping shared values from Enterprise to Coos Bay. Working-class connections reached widely across Oregon. The hinterland of Portland was a land of rugged loggers, mill hands, railroad crews, bindle-stiffs, gillnetters, and cannery workers. There were populists and socialists in Portland, radical Finnish immigrants in Astoria, and Wobblies organizing in the woods. Workers flowed back and forth across the state, migrating from one seasonal job to another. In his novel *Honey in the Horn* (1935), H. L. Davis looked back to the early years of the century, taking his protagonists back and forth across the state from mountains to coast to midlands, from sheep herding to horse breaking, from hop picking to hay making.

When farmers had their harvests in, when bad weather closed the logging camps and shut down railroad building, seasonal workers drifted into Portland, filling a bachelor neighborhood that stretched a mile along the downtown waterfront. They bought new gear, enjoyed clean beds before they drank up their wages, and ended up sleeping in a flophouse or in the back room of one of Portland's two hundred saloons. To find men without families, Portlanders needed only to follow loud music and the smell of stale beer to waterfront blocks between Everett and Jackson streets. From the Lownsdale district on the south to the Burnside district on the north, this Skid Road was a neighborhood of lodging houses and flophouses, secondhand stores, missions, saloons, brothels, and employment agencies. At its height between 1900 and 1925, the district may have housed as many as ten thousand men, giving Portland proportionately one of the largest skid roads in the country and linking it inextricably to the work of the hinterland.

At the same time, other Oregonians shared a business-oriented middle-class culture. The Ku Klux Klan found ready acceptance across the state in 1921 and 1922, organizing successfully in places as physically distant as Tillamook, Portland, Hood River, Eugene, Salem, Medford, Astoria, Pendleton, and La Grande. Klan sympathizers tended to be homeowners with stable roots in Oregon's smaller communities. The organization was intolerantly anti-immigrant and anti-Catholic, but many members, who ranged from successful businessmen to skilled workers, saw themselves as sharing a positive commitment to business-oriented Protestantism and the 1920s version of "family values."[3]

Klan voters from across the state helped to elect Walter Pierce of La Grande as governor in 1922. La Grande was the gubernatorial hometown most distant from the metropolis. Pierce's victory can be read as an example of the sharing of political leadership widely across the state during this period. The hometowns or home bases of all the governors elected between 1910 and 1939 were widely scattered. Governors certainly came from Salem (three times) and Portland (twice) but also from Condon, Astoria, Roseburg, Corvallis, Union County, and Polk County.

As late as the 1960s, patterns of political affiliation were similar across the different regions of the state. Data on Democrats as a proportion of all registered voters (see Chapter 7) show that the strongest contrast, that between the Middle Willamette Valley on the one hand and the North Coast and Multnomah County on the other hand, was no more than 10 percent for 1966-1970. The regional differences were enough for politicians to notice but not enough to generate talk about "two Oregons."

The Long Arm of the Metropolis

In the last four decades it has become necessary to think of the urban system in Oregon as centered not on a single city but on a dominant metropolitan region stretching from Portland (actually the region begins in Vancouver, Washington) to McMinnville and perhaps even through Salem (table 5). This emergent pattern raises definitional challenges, since the census uses counties as metro area components, and there are plenty of folks in Yamhill, Columbia, and Polk counties who don't think of themselves as metropolitan types, let alone Portlanders.[4]

As additional Oregon cities received metropolitan designation—Eugene in 1960, Salem in 1970, Medford in 1980, Bend and Corvallis in 2000—Portland's primate-city edge gave way to a more balanced urban system. The three-county core of the metropolitan area held a steady 40-42 percent of the state

1980		2000		2007 estimates	
Portland metro: three OR counties	1,050,418	Portland metro: five OR counties	1,572,701	Portland metro: five OR counties	1,734,020
Eugene metro	275,226	Salem metro	347,214	Salem metro	378,520
Salem metro	249,895	Eugene metro	322,955	Eugene metro	343,140
Medford metro	132,456	Medford metro	181,269	Medford metro	202,310
Corvallis	40,960	Bend metro	115,367	Bend metro	160,810

Table 5. Largest Oregon metropolitan areas and cities, 1980, 2000, and 2007 (estimates). Note: If the adjacent Corvallis Metropolitan Area and Albany Micropolitan Area were combined, to reflect the proximity and close ties between the two cities, their 2000 population would be 181,222, bumping in between Medford and Bend (see table 6). Sources: U.S. Census Bureau; Population Research Center, Portland State University.

population from 1950 to 2000. In 1960 these three counties were twice as large as the next twelve urban places. Because smaller cities have achieved the status of metro areas, the Portland metro area is now twice as large as only the next two metro areas, a position it has held since 1970.

The source of this changing pattern has been the relative rise of cities with economies based on information and leisure, namely the university, technology, and recreation cities of Eugene, Corvallis-Albany, and Bend (table 6). In 1880, Albany had claimed fifth rank and Corvallis eighth because of the expansion of mid-Willamette Valley farming. These cities had sagged to fifteenth and tenth places, respectively, by the onset of World War II, as cities like Medford, Klamath Falls, and Pendleton elbowed them toward the rear of the pack, but they recovered their earlier standing in the ensuing decades. Bend is a twentieth-century city that surged to seventh place in the 1930s on the basis of lumber and irrigated agriculture, fell back after the war, and has since climbed into the top five.

Many trends have shaped the new economic and metropolitan landscape, ranging from the emergence of new industries to the technological trans-formation of the wood-products industry. In addition to these long-cycle forces, however, Oregonians made an implicit deal in the 1970s with the adoption of a statewide system for land-use planning. Senate Bill 100, which established the system, passed with a partnership of Portland and Willamette Valley legislators who crafted what has turned out to be a policy of compact metropolitan growth, which has kept urban sprawl from overrunning the val-ley's vineyards, filbert orchards, and other specialized agricultural lands. The legislation passed with forty-nine of a possible sixty votes from Willamette Valley legislators but only nine of a possible thirty votes from their colleagues from coastal and eastern Oregon.

Portland's side of the implicit deal is to protect the farm economy and to continue to provide the facilities for selling rural products in world markets. Portland is the junction and transfer point for interstate highway trucking, rail cargo, Columbia and Snake river barge traffic, and international shipping.[5] Portland exports leisure-industry jobs and retiree transfer payments to coastal and central counties—places where resort and second-home development faces limitations intended to preserve the resource economy. Metropolitan taxes also subsidize downstate school systems and services.

Rural Oregon agrees, if reluctantly, under the deal to limits on forestry and conversion of resource land. The bargain is apparent in Hood River and

Metros		Micros	
Portland	1,572,701		
Salem	347,214		
Eugene	322,959		
Medford	181,269		
Bend	115,367		
		Albany	103,069
		Roseburg	100,399
		Pendleton	81,543
Corvallis	78,153		
		Grants Pass	75,726
		Klamath Falls	63,775
		Coos Bay	62,779
		Ontario	52,193
		Astoria	35,630
		La Grande	24,530
		The Dalles	23,791
		Brookings	21,137
		Hood River	20,411
		Prineville	19,182

Table 6. Population of Oregon metropolitan and micropolitan areas, 2000. Source: U.S. Census Bureau.

Wasco counties. The Columbia River Gorge National Scenic Area, for example, is a product of metro Portland political organizing, but the expectation is that the areas will benefit from protected agriculture, the rise of a leisure economy, and high-tech industry attracted by local amenities. There are high-tech sectors in Deschutes County and in the mid-Columbia counties, notably Google in The Dalles. Rural Oregon also gains from providing other services for the metropolis. Portland has trucked most of its solid waste to Gilliam County for two decades, filling deep ravines between the vast wheat fields. The growing number of prisoners in the contemporary "carceral society" (to use the social critic Michel Foucault's term) has required Oregon to open or expand ten prisons since 1985; only two have been in the Willamette Valley, while two have been on the coast and six in eastern Oregon.[6]

Although not part of the tacit bargain, rural Oregon also benefits from the fact that Portland itself sits relatively lightly on the landscape. Metropolitan

Portland now grows much more compactly than most other U.S. cities. From 1980 to 1994, metropolitan population increased by 25 percent, while the land devoted to urban uses increased by only 16 percent. (In contrast, population in the Chicago area rose 4 percent from 1970 to 1990, and urbanized land increased by 46 percent.) In 1994 the Portland area was building new housing at a density of five dwelling units per acre. By 1998 the density of new development averaged eight dwellings per acre, actually exceeding the ambitious target of the regional 2040 Plan. The average new-lot size by 1998 was 6,200 square feet, down from 12,800 square feet in 1978 (Metro, Growth Management Section, unpublished data). Until these recent changes in development patterns, the Portland region was growing more compactly than many other metropolitan regions (i.e., with contiguous rather than scattered development), but not more densely (i.e., in terms of population per square mile). In 2000, the urbanized areas of the Portland-Vancouver metro area—the actual acreage devoted to buildings, roads, city parks, and other clearly urban land uses—totaled 474 square miles, or 0.005 percent of Oregon's total land area. Because the figure includes the urbanized part of Clark County, Washington, the direct impact on Oregon is even less. Adding in the urbanized areas of Salem (69 square miles), Eugene (68 square miles), and Medford (58 square miles) ups the coverage to only 0.007 percent of the state.

Oregon's climate and landscape also allow Portland and suburban communities to reach relatively short distances for resources to sustain the metropolitan metabolism. Sand and gravel for construction are available from local river deposits. Water for homes and industry comes roughly fifty miles from the Coast Range and Mount Hood, not from hundreds of miles away, as for Los Angeles, or across the Continental Divide, as for Denver. The Columbia River and its tributaries—and now the windswept bluffs of the Columbia Plateau—provide a large proportion of metropolitan electricity. In total, the metropolitan footprints of Portland and other Willamette Valley cities are much less than those of Los Angeles or Phoenix, and thus impinge less on rural and small-town Oregon.

It is not clear that perceptions have caught up with realities. Ask an Oregonian to name the novelists who have best dealt with post-World War II Oregon, and we would expect the list to include Craig Lesley, David James Duncan, Robin Cody, and Ken Kesey. These are all skilled and perceptive writers, but the Oregon they portray is the Oregon of the 1950s, not the Oregon of the twenty-first century. Their characters live in a state where logging, farming, and the wood-products industry dominate community life. Home for them is Bend and Pendleton, Estacada, Camas (which is not in Oregon, of course, but it's a near neighbor and a mirror of Oregon towns like St. Helens), and a place something like Waldport. Big cities are absent in Lesley's work, figure as a realm that destabilizes community in Cody's *Ricochet River,* house insensitive bureaucracies in Duncan's *The Brothers K,* and trouble Hank Stamper with the demands of labor unions in Kesey's *Sometimes a Great Notion.* We're still waiting for the U.S. version of Douglas Coupland, the Canadian writer and author of the bestseller *Generation X,* to skewer contemporary Portland and place it on the same specimen tray with Vancouver, Palm Springs, Seattle, and San Jose.

Voters, however, may be a more sensitive indicator than novelists. Votes on early efforts to undo the state land-use system—Measure 10 in 1976, Measure 6 in 1982—show the traditional division in which the Willamette Valley lined up against the coast and southern and eastern Oregon. By the 1990s, though, more of the state's northwestern quadrant was voting the same way as Portland on statewide races and ballot measures related to social and cultural values, as measured by county majorities. In 1992, for example, the northern coast (Lincoln, Tillamook, and Clatsop counties), metropolitan Portland, the central valley counties of Lane and Benton, the north-central counties (Hood River, Wasco, Sherman, Gilliam, and Deschutes), and two southern counties (Coos and Jackson) all rejected Measure 9, which would have allowed discrimination on the basis of sexual orientation.

Fast-forward another decade and a half to 2007 and things really begin to get interesting for Oregon historians. The vote on Measure 49, which mitigated some of the stronger provisions in the very strong 2004 property-rights initiative, Measure 37, suggests that the basic political and cultural division in Oregon does not pit east side against west side or the Willamette Valley against everyone else. Instead, the division seems to be between southern-tier counties and the rest of the state. As a proposal to soften the impact of Measure 37, Measure 49 rolled back the wholesale granting of retroactive real estate development rights while confirming "retail" or "family-scale" rights. The change resulted from increased understanding of the practical consequences of Measure 37 in many areas not heavily impacted by development pressures. It appealed to Union County residents who didn't want to see the Grande Ronde Valley filled with a thousand transplanted Californians, to Hood River residents who didn't want to see development replace orchards on the entire east side of the valley, to suburbanites who worried about sprawl, and to farmers who didn't want to see subdivisions popping up among vineyards and mint fields. Opposition to Measure 49 was strongest in a solid southern tier from Curry, Coos, and Douglas counties to Harney and Malheur counties. Measure 49 either passed or came in with 49 percent positive votes across the rest of the state with the exceptions of Sherman and Grant counties.[7]

Conclusion

We may be seeing a new twist on the old story of city and hinterland. Portland—and Salem and Eugene and Corvallis—may now be exporting metropolitan culture along with retirees and recreationists. A metropolitan "weekendland" extends from Newport to Bend to Hood River and back to Astoria. Far larger than the familiar metropolitan areas defined by daily commuting, this is a region that retains much of its rural or semi-rural landscape but is increasingly tied to the Willamette Valley by weekly visitation and tele-commuting. In the years just before the 2007 real estate crash, for example, roughly 30 percent of the residential mortgages in Deschutes County and along the northern Oregon coast (45 percent in Tillamook County) were for second homes. In turn, the rise of recreation industries helps to attract mi-grants directly from out-of-state metropolitan areas to places like Hood River, further urbanizing local culture. Will Oregon be entering a fourth era of city-country relationships and interaction in the 2010s and 2020s? Historians are not necessarily experts at predicting the future, but my bets are on a continu-ing convergence that gradually bridges the differences and divides of the late twentieth century.

Bibliography

Bryce, James. 1888. "The Temper of the West." *The American Commonwealth*. New York: Macmillan.

Chalmers, David. 1987. *Hooded Americanism: The History of the Ku Klux Klan*. Durham, N.C.: Duke University Press.

Cody, Robin. 2005. *Ricochet River*. Portland: Ooligan Press.

Coupland, Douglas. 1991. *Generation X: Tales for an Accelerated Culture*. New York: St. Martin's Press.

Croly, Herbert D. 1912. "Portland, Oregon: The transformation of the city from an architectural and social viewpoint." *Architectural Record* 31 (June): 592.

Davis, H. L. 1935. *Honey in the Horn*. New York: Harper and Brothers.

Day and Zimmerman, Inc. 1930. *Survey of Industrial Activities and Resources and of the Proposed Establishment of an Industrial District in Portland, Oregon*. Portland.

Duncan, David James. 1992. *The Brothers K*. New York: Doubleday.

"The future of north coast cities." 1909. *World's Work* 11945 (August 1909), 18.

Hungerford, Edward. 1913. *The Personality of American Cities*. New York: McBride, Nast and Co.

Jackson, Kenneth T. 1967. *The Ku Klux Klan in the City, 1915-1930*. New York: Oxford University Press.

Kesey, Ken. 1964. *Sometimes a Great Notion*. New York: Viking Press.

Kipling, Rudyard. 1899. *From Sea to Sea*. New York: Doubleday.

Loy, William G., Stuart Allan, Aileen Buckley, and Jim Meacham. 2001. *Atlas of Oregon*. Eugene: University of Oregon Press.

McKenzie, Roderick. 1933. *The Metropolitan Community*. New York and London: McGraw-Hill.

Moore, Leonard J. 1991. *Citizen Klansmen: The Ku Klux Klan in Indiana*. Chapel Hill: University of North Carolina Press.

The Oregonian, 1910. Special Jan. 1 issue.

The Oregonian, 1919. Jan. 1 and Oct. 19 issues.

The Oregonian, 1920. Jan. 1 issue.

Ralph, Julian. 1893. *Our Great West: A Study of the Present Conditions and Future Possibilities of New Capitals of the United States*. New York: Harper and Brothers.

Reserve Bank Organization Committee. 1914. *Decision of the Reserve Bank Organization Committee Determining the Federal Reserve Districts and the Location of Federal Reserve Banks under Federal Reserve Act Approved December 23, 1913, April 2, 1914, with Statement of the Committee in Relation Thereto, April 10, 1914*. Washington, D.C.: Government Printing Office.

Reserve Bank Organization Committee. [Undated] *Letters from the Reserve Bank Organizing Committee Transmitting the Briefs and Arguments Presented to the Organization Committee of the Federal Reserve Board Relative to the Location of Reserve Districts in the United States*. Senate Document 485, 63d Cong., 2nd Sess., 349-57.

Sensenisch, Edgar. 1918. *Bankers' Magazine* 97 (November): 654.

Thayer, William. 1887. *Marvels of the New West: A Vivid Portrayal of the Stupendous Marvels of the Vast Wonderland West of the Missouri River*. Norwich, Conn.: The Henry Bill Publishing Co.

Chapter 4
Town and Country in Oregon
A Conflicted Legacy
William G. Robbins

The landscapes of the American and Canadian West offer great distances between towns, a lower intensity and volume of human activity than in the East, and, in many places, abandoned farmsteads and town sites. In his bestseller *Great Plains*, the writer Ian Frazier provides a blunt assessment of that West: "Money and power in this country concentrate elsewhere" (Frazier 1989). The poet and essayist Kathleen Norris referred to Dakota's west-river country as "a school for humility," where people's "inability to influence either big business or big government is turning all Dakotans into a kind of underclass" (Norris 1993). Because the High Plains has always been a sparsely settled place with few urban centers, it has long been customary to characterize its relationship to the rest of the nation as colonial. It is not unique, however, because the region is at one with significant portions of other western states, a region that the journalist Joel Garreau once described as "the Empty Quarter" (Garreau 1981).

Sixty years ago, Carey McWilliams, arguably California's greatest twentieth-century writer, suggested that, for most of its history, California has been the urban center for the area west of the Continental Divide (McWilliams 1949, 82). The coastal reaches of California represented all that the word "metropolis" brings to mind—images of power and influence, a centeredness to things, seats of business and cultural institutions. Oregon, with its major metropolitan center in the lower Willamette Valley and its vast, lightly populated interior region, represents a microcosm of California and its relations with states on the Pacific slope. From the time of the California Gold Rush, the Oregon outback and adjacent areas have also served as a literal treasure house of resources for the expanding industrial appetites of Atlantic-centered nation states. What is fascinating about America's Far West is the spectacular scope and rapid pace of change during the last century and a half.

The roots of that dramatic transformation can be best understood within the broader context of the ever-shifting world of modern capitalism—its propensity for technological dynamism and endless innovation, and its relentless pursuit of new marketing opportunities and new sources of raw material and labor. Because capitalism became the organizing principle for much of the world economy following the Industrial Revolution, it provides the most systematic framework for explaining change in the American West and the region's integration into national and international exchange relations. Oregon's development over the last one hundred fifty years, therefore, has never occurred in isolation from broader currents of national and global economic activity. Rather, Oregon and the greater West have moved in concert with larger trade and capital exchanges, relationships that vastly accelerated with the coming of steel rails to the region.

The emergence of urban centers in the American West and their association with extensive hinterlands also developed in tandem with investment and marketing initiatives often originating far from the region itself. The political philosopher Marshall Berman argued that the principal force driving the "maelstrom of modern life" at the close of the nineteenth century was the "ever-expanding, drastically fluctuating world market." That far-reaching global system, he observed, was "capable of appalling waste and devastation, capable of everything except solidity and stability" (Berman 1982, 16, 19).[1] In that sense, the late-nineteenth-century American West was a prototype for modern capitalism, providing a warehouse of natural resources and an investment arena for eastern U.S. and European capital—and suffering dramatic plunges in the business cycle when corporate moguls withdrew their investments.

As a methodology for studying Western history, relations between country and city provide important insights into the spatial distribution of power and influence. Although the urban-hinterland relationship poses many questions, it still provides useful ideas for understanding power relationships within the West and with more distant centers of capital.[2] Fernand Braudel, the distinguished French historian, put the case succinctly when he compared center and peripheral areas, in which the latter were "subordinates rather than true participants" in decision making.[3] There were, he observed, "increasingly fewer advantages as one moves out from the triumphant pole" (Braudel 1977,

82-85). Braudel raised a fundamental question about that relationship: the lack of autonomy in the countryside. The persistence of protest in the rural West—from the Populists of the 1890s to the county-sovereignty movement of the last twenty years—provides ideological strength to the rural-urban distinction.

The use of urban-hinterland relationships is not meant to suggest that these are unchanging, static categories; they are dynamic, always in the process of readjustment, but they still represent categories of the more powerful and the less powerful. Although the volume of scholarly work on urban-hinterland relations has multiplied in the last few decades, most of the debates have involved Third World dependency issues. Until recently, scholars have given little consideration to those questions within the United States.[4]

Most historians have viewed the American West prior to World War II as a colonial sector, subordinate to distant metropolitan-based economies. With the growth of early urban centers in the West—San Francisco, Portland, and Denver—the region developed its own centers of influence, each with ties to its own tributary hinterlands. The environmental historian William Cronon observed that city and countryside were never isolated but shared common features, with the former benefiting from profits accruing to its banking and mortgage houses (Cronon 1991, 7-8). The geographer Michael Conzen portrayed the nature of that relationship: "The larger the city, the wider its horizons, and the more elaborate its set of hinterlands" (Conzen 1977, 89). The stunning rapidity of resettlement in the West[5] and the development of vibrant resource-based economics paralleled the emergence of the United States as a global power. The region's growing urban centers and their resource-rich hinterlands were critical to the successes of the Atlantic industrial world.

During this period, Oregon and the American West were being incorporated into the expanding world of industrial capitalism at a time when the global economy was becoming truly capitalistic. Investors representing centers of surplus capital were literally traveling the far corners of the globe looking for investment opportunities. With its prodigious fish runs, valuable mineral deposits, rich agricultural lands, and abundant stands of timber, the Pacific Northwest represented great promise to investors. The ideology driving that rush of investment focused on transforming western landscapes into wealth-producing instruments. The antecedents to Oregon's modern places, therefore, are best understood in terms of national and global conditions that powered the dynamics of change.

Rural sectors of western America were negatively affected in still other ways, especially by technological advances in transportation and communication that favored expanding urban centers. San Francisco, Portland, and Seattle all developed extensive tributary hinterlands by virtue of advantages in location, entrepreneurial drive, and capacity to process and market natural resources. While San Francisco was the standard-bearer in extending the reach of capital into the countryside, lesser metropoles such as Portland were part of that story. Colonialism, as many scholars have demonstrated, is both an internal and an external phenomenon. Although Portland merchants had significant ties to their more powerful counterparts in San Francisco, by virtue of their own capital assets and ties to local banking houses they were in a commanding position in the Willamette and Columbia river corridors. The division between dominant and dominated economies, therefore, extends from subregions of the nation-state to the greater capitalist world economy, a set of relationships that prevails to the present day.[6]

Portland has arguably been the driving force in Oregon's economy since its early days, when it was informally known as Stumptown, capturing the trade of the Willamette Valley and shipping wheat and other grain products to oceanic markets. The historian Carlos Schwantes points out that Portland was the only Northwest settlement to develop into a city before the arrival of transcontinental railroads. Its harbor provided sufficient draft for deep-water ships, and its waterfront was piled high with "lumber, wheat, fruit, and other farm products . . . for distant markets." When the Ladd and Tilton Bank opened in 1859 and the telegraph reached the city in 1864, Portland solidified its status as the region's preeminent financial center. Booming interior mining camps in the 1860s boosted the city's prosperity, its steamboats monopolizing traffic on the Columbia River. "Gold and wheat made Portland rich and smug by the late 1870s," Schwantes writes, "a place untroubled . . . and not a little complacent in its role as the region's premier metropolis" (Schwantes 1996, 236).

With its built environment on the west side of the Willamette River about twelve miles above its junction with the Columbia, Portland had a population of 2,874 in 1860, three times that of any other settlement in the Northwest (Dicken and Dicken 1979, 81 and 92). Plank roads built to rich prairie lands west and south of town during the 1850s contributed mightily to Portland's preeminence on the Willamette (Winther 1950, 124). *The Oregonian* boasted in 1867 that Portland was "more distinctively a commercial city" than any other community in the state, exhibiting the signs of maturity and domination over an expanding tributary region. The regional booster publication *West Shore* labeled Portland "the Oregon Emporium" because it had captured the trade of its interior at the time of the California Gold Rush. The city's business community worked to connect "the external commerce of the country," *West Shore* reported, "to bring the prairie schooner and the ocean-going vessel together" (*West Shore* 1875, 4). Those booster narratives failed to mention that Portland's Front Street merchants—William Ladd, Josiah Failing, and A. M. Starr—raised most of the money to extend the city's growing infrastructure.

Portland grew apace in size and influence, developing a trading network that fronted in two directions, outward to oceanic markets and sources of capital, and inward via the Willamette and Columbia corridors to a vast, resource-rich hinterland. Beyond the exaggerated claims of its boosters, Portland was actually an intermediary settlement, a medium for exchange between distant centers of capital and its own outback. In that reciprocal relationship, mercantile shops and warehouses in smaller interior communities paid tribute to Portland, just as the city's merchants and bankers paid tribute to coastwide merchants in San Francisco. Although Stumptown was a mere village compared to the Bay Area metropolis, the historian Dorothy Johansen aptly described Portland "as the 'city that gravity built.' Down the Willamette flowed the produce of the Valley; down the Columbia came the immigrants and the riches of Idaho mines and interior wheat fields" (Johansen 1967, 279). In each exchange, California ships delivered materials and supplies for distribution to the Willamette Valley and to sternwheelers plying the waters of the Columbia.

In the midst of the expanding commerce on the region's rivers, John C. Ainsworth, Simeon G. Reed, and Robert R. Thompson pooled their financial resources in 1860 to form the region's first business monopoly, the Oregon Steam Navigation Company (OSN) (Johansen 1967). The OSN was a $5 million operation by the late 1860s, managing water and land routes far into the interior Columbia drainage. Controlling portages on the river at the Cascades and above The Dalles was the key to OSN's success. To facilitate passage around the rapids and falls, the company built a six-mile railroad around the Cascades of the Columbia and a fourteen-mile railroad around The Dalles.

Although it operated powerful and fashionable sternwheelers and moved a huge volume of passengers and freight the company's monopoly provoked widespread discontent in eastern Oregon and in Washington Territory. Baker

City's *Bedrock Democrat* described the company as "a positive curse to East-ern Oregon, Idaho, and Washington Territories." The OSN's owners were guilty of "overreaching avarice" and were "codfish aristocrats, . . . sordid and grasping" (Johansen 1941, 258). The Portland historian E. Kimbark MacColl provides an appropriate summary of the company's influence: "Luxurious passenger service and monopolistic freight rates created and sustained the veritable cash machine that was bitterly resented by the eastern Oregon mer-chants and farmers" (MacColl 1988, 207).

Because the San Francisco market dominated Portland's wheat exports, lo-cal merchants attempted to make themselves independent of the coastal mar-ket and began shipping wheat directly to Liverpool, England, in 1869. With Portland merchants controlling all agricultural exports from the Willamette Valley, Corvallis-area entrepreneurs, backed by British capital, also pursued a short-lived attempt in the 1870s—via a proposed railroad from Corvallis to the East—to circumvent Portland's monopoly control of export markets for agricultural products from the Willamette Valley. With an engaging southern colonel, T. Egenton Hogg, as front man, the company completed a railroad from Corvallis west through the Coast Range to Yaquina Bay and then east to Albany in 1886 (Johansen 1967, 282).[7] With ambitions to build a transconti-nental link across the Cascades, Hogg's construction crews reached the small settlement of Idanha at the end of the 1880s, still fifteen miles from Santiam Pass. At that point the company went bankrupt, and the mid-valley dream of being free of Portland merchants and bankers collapsed.

As for Portland's boosters, they believed that railroads were the transcen-dent vehicle to the city's success. As a proud symbol of industrial capitalism, railroads represented an aggressive move to take advantage of the region's natural bounty. According to *The Oregonian* (1865), this new revolutionary means of transportation would prove "an indispensable adjunct of civiliza-tion." Portland promoters saw themselves at the epicenter of rail construction to and from the city, the recipient of the wealth of a bounteous hinterland (MacColl 1988, 250). Beyond the lower Willamette metropolis, others were more cautious about the benefits that a railroad would bring. Jesse Applegate, an early settler in the upper Umpqua Valley, worried that a proposed route from Portland to Sacramento might "bind us in vassalage to our strong neigh-bor [San Francisco] forever" (*The Oregonian* 1863).

Only weeks before the Northern Pacific line reached Portland in 1883, *The Oregonian* predicted that isolated upriver sections of the continent would soon be sending their products to "River City" (*The Oregonian*, Aug. 14, 1883). With the passage of time, the newspaper's booster narrative assumed dream-like proportions, arguing that Portland's physical location at the "Railroad Crossroads" of the Pacific Northwest would attract the region's business just as "the physical law which makes water run down hill." Portlanders were ambitious, as *The Oregonian* put it in a celebratory New Year's issue in 1888, believing that the wealth of "eastern and Western Oregon, eastern Washington and Idaho" would pour into the city's "expanding clasp," bringing "a larger share of commercial profit and substantial wealth to the city" (*The Oregonian*, Jan. 2, 1888). By the early twentieth century, Portland-based trade publications would far surpass *The Oregonian* in anticipating the wealth that would flow to the growing settlement on the lower Willamette.

Inherent in the dynamic alterations to the region's landscape, however, were growing tensions between metropolis and hinterland, between city and country, between expanding urban centers and rural spatial zones beyond—areas chiefly important for the goods they shipped to the metropolis. Oregon provides an abundance of testimony to the influence of financial, social, and political power. That story had begun to assume its modern form with the building of the Oregon and California Railroad south from Portland in the early 1870s. For the Willamette and Umpqua valleys the new mode of transportation initiated a shift from subsistence to commercial agriculture, raising land values, introducing a cornucopia of mass-produced farm equipment, and—most important to this discussion—fomenting anger against the exploitative practices of the railroad and Portland banking and mortgage houses.

The completion of the Oregon and California Railroad provides a modest textbook example of the conflicts that flared between rural producers and merchants, banking houses, and especially railroads—the mode of transportation that made commercial farming enterprises possible.[8] The confrontation erupted shortly after the tracks reached Roseburg in the fall of 1872, with farmers accusing local merchants and the railroad of working in collusion to deprive them of the just profits of their labor. They charged merchants with making secret agreements with the railroad to raise shipping rates on grain crops and the wool clip. With the same broadsides, farmers attacked Portland bankers for lending practices that discriminated against rural citizens. In response to these practices, Umpqua Valley sheep ranchers formed the Wool Growers' Association to protect against monopolies "detrimental to the interest of the producing and laboring classes" (Roseburg *Plaindealer* 1873), an initiative that led directly to the organization of Umpqua Grange, Number 29, in 1873.

The Grangers (Patrons of Husbandry) represented the advance wave of rural protest movements that spread across agricultural sections of the United States in the 1870s in response to the increasing corporatization of the American economy. Other movements followed: the Farmers' Alliances in the 1880s, the Populist challenge in the mid-1890s, and continuing insurgencies in the first two decades of the twentieth century. Rural people who participated in those remonstrations pursued railroad regulation (even government ownership), greater equity in tax policy, and the formation of marketing cooperatives and other collaborative enterprises to contend with volatile market conditions. When the United States descended into its first large-scale industrial depression in 1893, agrarian reformers formed short-lived alliances with industrial laborers in a common cause against the forces of capital, both identifying themselves as members of the "productive classes" (Watkins 1995, 12; Danbom 1995).

Grangers across the Pacific Northwest formed cooperative stores, warehouses, and grain elevators to eliminate middleman costs and to give themselves a stronger position in the marketplace. Although the cooperative schemes enjoyed occasional successes, lack of capital, inexperienced management, opposition from financial institutions, and aggressive competing businesses caused most of them to fail (Danbom 1995, 154-55; Watkins 1995, 184-85).[9] Although the Grange declined as an effective agrarian political institution in the Midwest, it remained a significant player in Oregon and Washington politics until World War I. Like the Populists, the Grange offered a critique of capitalism that advocated protecting small landholders and subjecting large land ownerships, transportation systems, and financial institutions to government regulation or ownership. The strength of the collective forces of capital—banking institutions, railroads, the emergence of commodity exchanges, and other related factors—explains the failure of the Grange to effectively address agrarian problems.

Although those late nineteenth-century rural insurgencies varied in temper and ideology, Marilyn Watkins argues, in her study of western Washington's Lewis County, that farmers "shared the goal of securing government protection from the vagaries of an international capitalist economy and the abuses of industrial corporations." Because they envisioned "a cooperative commonwealth" where producing classes enjoyed "the fruits of their labor and justice prevailed," Lewis County's farmers supported the Populists in the early 1890s (Watkins 1995, 4, 67). In southern Oregon's Jackson County—another center of rural discontent during the 1890s—farmers protested railroad and flour-mill monopoly, inequitable taxes, and the low prices they received for their orchard crops. The Jacksonville *Democrat Times* declared in December 1891: "[T]his is a struggle of the people against plutocracy" (LaLande 1993, 21, 29, 36, 45). Jackson County gave Populist candidate James B. Weaver a plurality of the presidential vote in 1892 and overwhelmingly supported the Democratic-Populist fusion candidate, William Jennings Bryan, for president in 1896.

The dimensions of rural protest in early twentieth-century Oregon adjusted to changes taking place in the greater world of American capitalism, especially state and federal moves toward regulating corporate behavior. Although Democratic gubernatorial candidate Sylvester Pennoyer called for regulating railroad rates as early as 1886, the Oregon legislature moved haltingly, creating an ineffective Board of Railroad Commissioners in 1887 and then abolishing it in 1898. Joseph Simon, a Portland railroad lawyer and senate president, led the move to abolish the commission. Agrarian interests finally achieved a modest victory in 1907 when Oregon lawmakers reestablished a railroad commission with limited regulatory power. The commission's principal contribution was to gather and publish information on interstate railroads, especially the great profitability of some lines (MacColl 1988; Johansen 1967). Because the revamped commission provided farmers with data about excessive profiteering, their protests about inequitable railroad rates and warehouse and grain elevator charges would continue.

Resistance of another kind emerged in the early twentieth century, largely from rural sectors of Oregon, with crosscurrents of cooperation between Grangers and organized labor. Rural opposition to Progressive Era reforms emerged, however, when urban dwellers initiated reforms designed to open public *and* private lands to resource production and to impose state regulations on taking fish and wildlife.[10] An even more acrimonious divisiveness between rural and urban constituencies involved state initiatives to use tax monies to build a scenic highway through the Columbia River Gorge. Those contentious issues involved class and cultural differences, productive versus leisure use of resources, and differences over the appropriate use of tax revenue. Both farmers and urban workers were fearful that the unregulated market and the overweening influence of corporate power would increase inequality in American life, with agrarian and urban people reduced to vassalage.

The reformer William S. U'Ren, the principal architect of Oregon's system of direct democracy—the initiative, referendum, recall, and direct election of U.S. senators—included among his closest allies the Oregon State Grange, the Farmers Union, and the state Federation of Labor (Johnston 2003). The roots of that collaboration date from the mid-1890s and the formation of the Joint Committee on Direct Legislation. While writers have focused on U'Ren's effort to establish direct democracy to curtail the influence of big money in politics, the historian Lawrence Lipin argues that his larger objective was to have voters enact Henry George's single tax, a maneuver "that would have taxed nonproductive, speculatively held real estate out of existence." Despite present-day conservative abuses of the initiative process, Lipin contends that Oregonians should thank "this anti-corporate spirit" for bringing direct democracy to the state's polity (Lipin 2007, 10).

U'Ren's ideas appealed to many in the Oregon State Grange and the Farmers Union who opposed monopoly ownership of valuable timber and agricultural land. His People's Power League also introduced several initiatives to eliminate the Oregon senate and create a unicameral legislative system with proportional representation. The Grange and the Farmers Union supported the measures, believing that abolishing the senate—which they saw as representing the monied classes, corruption, and inefficiency in government—would return political power to the people (Lipin 2007, 41). Opponents of the unicameral-legislature proposal, most of whose leadership resided in Portland, accused the People's Power League of promoting "crackpot" proposals. *The Oregonian* called such measures "U'Renisms" (Johnston 2003, 142). Although populist measures such as unicameralism and proportional representation failed, they reflected voters' unease about the influence of money in politics.

A 1912 initiative that would apply a graduated income tax on large landholdings illustrates the producer-oriented, anti-corporate politics behind this period of rural and urban working-class cooperation. Sponsored by the Graduated Single Tax League of Oregon, the measure proposed to abolish the large speculative land ownerships of "railroads and other franchise corporations; by the land speculators, including the great landlords in Portland, and by the owners of valuable water powers" (Lipin 2007, 24). Although voters overwhelmingly defeated the initiative, it found considerable favor in the Oregon countryside, where there was widespread antagonism against railroad land grants. Targeting monopoly land ownership and those who held land only for its speculative value, single-tax supporters argued that such property should be put to productive use for the benefit of the larger community.

The rural and urban workers' struggle against land monopoly assumed even more radical overtones in a proposed constitutional amendment in 1916, the Full Rental Value Land Tax and Homemakers' Loan Fund Amendment. U'Ren drafted the initiative in the midst of a depression, with the objective of attacking "all the predatory interests, all the big business interests speculating in land" (Johnston 2003, 172). In his view, the measure, a tax on large land-holdings, would empower "all useful labor . . . laborers, clerks [and] farmers" (Johnston 2003, 173), providing them with an opportunity to make a living for themselves and their families. In the end, voters turned back the efforts of Oregon's home-grown radicals to institute various single-tax proposals. The 1916 Land and Loan measure lost in a landslide, with 75 percent of Portlanders voting against it. Voters statewide defeated the measure even more soundly, with 78 percent opposing. A tax system that relied on revenue from land value was obviously troubling to agrarian interests. Although similar measures were on the ballot in 1920 and 1922, voters rejected them with even larger margins. "The single tax," Robert Johnston writes, "finally died in Oregon" (Johnston 2003, 176).

Oregon's Progressive Era reforms introduced other changes to rural Oregon in the form of new state policies regulating the taking of fish and game. With automobiles providing middle- and upper-class citizens with greater access to the Oregon outback, the state legislature created the position of state game warden in 1911 and followed with a Fish and Game Commission to enforce increasingly restrictive laws on poachers. For rural people long accustomed to "living off the land," the new enforcement policies threatened their livelihoods. But the emergence of what Lipin calls "antielite politics" in the second decade of the twentieth century challenged the prerogatives of privileged urbanites who considered poachers the dregs of society. Agricultural interests—Grangers and the Farmers Union—and commercial fishers, who were organized into the Columbia River Fishermen's Protective Union, fought long and hard against sportsmen who wanted fish and game resources protected for leisure and recreational use. The Grange, in particular, opposed all game regulations, charging that such laws benefited the wealthy leisured class at the expense of hard-working farmers (Lipin 2007, 10-12, 49-52).

The differences between rural interests and organizations such as the Oregon Sportsmen's League, the Multnomah Anglers Club, and the Portland Commercial Club reflected class resentment against "the leisure class." When Grangers addressed fish and game regulations, Lipin contends, their public comments expressed indignation "against a largely urban-dominated state apparatus, of hardworking producers . . . and of small independent populist sorts up against powerful capitalist interests." At the annual meetings of the state Grange, members called for "the enactment of stringent trespass laws and that all farmers and stockmen be authorized to make arrests for the violation of same." At the same time, some local wardens and other rural officials ignored troublesome game laws, perhaps out of sympathy for their neighbors (Lipin 2007, 61).

Finally, opposition to funding and building the Columbia River Highway and other scenic byways created a parallel discourse, opposing the Grange and rural interests and the labor movement against "autoists" and the urban "leisure class." Wealthy Portland lumbermen Simon Benson and John Yeon, Great Northern Railway's Samuel Hill, and good-roads advocate Samuel Lancaster led the crusade to build the now-historic Columbia River Highway. When the proponents exhausted their funding and placed a bond measure on the ballot to pay for paving the highway, Portland's *Labor Press* pointed out that the road had no functional purpose other than to line the pockets of those who catered to tourism. The master of the Oregon State Grange, C. E. Spence, denounced the project as little more than "a pleasure road," an undertaking that would "place a mortgage on the homes of all the people to gratify a desire for joy riding." Appearing before the Oregon State Federation of Labor meeting in 1914, he pleaded "for good roads for the farmers instead of scenic highways for joy riders" (Lipin 2007, 38-41).

With the passing years, especially as the number of motorists increased and the Oregon Highway Commission funded the expansion of roadways to the farthest corners of the state, the rabid opposition to road building dissipated. Henry Ford's genius eventually placed the potential of automobile ownership in the hands of most working people. With diminishing passion for the single tax and the increasing number of drivers on the public highways, the old insurgent constituencies—Grangers, their rural allies, including the truly radical Nonpartisan League, and the Oregon State Federation of Labor—turned their energies in the 1920s to promoting a progressive income tax. With the Nonpartisan League and the Grange leading the way, organized labor joined the long struggle to establish a state income tax, a measure finally achieved in 1929. Lipin provides a fitting conclusion to a remarkable twenty-year period of agrarian-labor cooperation: "Leaving behind U'Ren's single tax, organized labor fell in behind the Grange's more electorally viable income tax measures" (Lipin 2007, 117, 147-52).

The years of the Great Depression and the tumultuous period of World War II fuzzed some of the differences between rural and urban America. The chase after mere survival during the 1930s left people struggling with sporadic and part-time employment or low-wage work with New Deal agencies such as the Civilian Conservation Corps and the Works Progress Administration. Still others survived by scouring the countryside, seeking recourse in old subsistence and foraging activities—berrying, cutting firewood, and bringing home fish and wild game. A remarkable study commissioned by President Herbert Hoover at the onset of his presidency underscored the problems of rural America. A massive tome of fifteen hundred pages of detailed scholarship, *Recent Social Trends in the United States* was released in 1933, shortly after Hoover had departed from office. Those who carefully read the document, the historian David Kennedy observes, "worried obsessively about 'balance' between rural and urban America," an issue the report referred to as the nation's "central problem" (Kennedy 1999, 10-12, 20-21). The Hoover study indicated that the great riches of the 1920s had gone disproportionately to the wealthy.

While those disparities persisted through the 1930s, the years of World War II transformed glutted job markets into labor scarcity after 1940. Those new conditions were heady experiences for people who had suffered more than a decade without steady work. Thousands of Oregonians left ranches and farms for defense plants in Portland, Seattle, and San Francisco, an exodus of people to urban centers that reshuffled the state's demographics. Many of Oregon's rural counties, especially those east of the Cascade Range, lost population during and after the war. The global conflict meant sharp increases in lumber and agricultural production, conditions that accelerated the transition to mechanized processes, with gasoline- and diesel-powered tractors replacing horses, oxen, and mules on farms and ranches. Those technological innovations—including a parallel mechanization in timber harvesting—revolutionized life in the Oregon outback.

To tell the story of the modern age, the British writer Eric Hobsbawm (1995) urged historians "to concentrate on the global transformation," especially following World War II, when the world capitalist economy centered on the United States. The boom that took place was unprecedented, with vast internal migrations from country to city, from rural environments to more promising opportunities in the metropolis. Of all the dramatic changes in the twentieth century, few were more significant than the dramatic population movement from rural to urban areas (Wood 2008, 3). This most striking demographic movement in modern American history was most apparent in California, whose vibrant market provided resource-dependent Oregon with a rapidly expanding outlet for wood products and agricultural goods. The boom broadened in the late 1940s, accelerated in the 1950s, and then reached unprecedented growth during the 1960s. Oregon's prewar economy—centered in agricultural and forest-related work—remained dominant in the immediate postwar years, with the state's forest industries employing more than 60 percent of "factory workers," in the Census Bureau's designation (U.S. Bureau of the Census 1940, 886, and 1950, 37-129; McKinley 1952, 10).

World War II had far-reaching effects on the Northwest forest-products industry and its dependent communities. After a decade and more of market-induced unemployment, Oregon's forested districts entered a period of sustained expansion, full employment, and regular paydays.[11] Oregon was the most timber-dependent state in the nation after World War II, with more than two thousand large and small lumbering and logging operations in 1947 and a combined payroll exceeding all other employment sectors. Domestic savings accumulated during the war precipitated three decades of booming construction activity, providing good-paying jobs for rural communities into the 1970s. For most people, life was good. Receipts from Forest Service and Bureau of Land Management timber sales kept county revenues flush and taxes low, and provided expanding road systems, good schools, and adequate county services for dependent counties.

Smaller Oregon communities from Coos Bay to Grants Pass, Roseburg, Bend, and Baker were alive and humming with activity. In Coos County on Oregon's southern coast, new mills opened, gyppo operators multiplied, and workers flocked to the area. Coos County's population grew more than 30 percent in the 1940s and 1950s, percentage increases comparable to California's during those two decades. A heady optimism prevailed around the Coos Bay communities, with some boosters predicting that the good times would last forever (Robbins 2006). Although there were occasional market-induced downturns during the 1950s and 1960s, workers always looked forward to renewed building activity, second shifts, overtime in the mills, and daybreak-to-dusk logging operations. Even in the darkest of winter months, everyone knew that the slackening of the seasonal rains would bring brighter job prospects. Economic conditions on the south coast—and in Oregon's other timber districts—were still relatively healthy through the 1960s and 1970s. But workers also witnessed ominous signs: accelerated harvesting rates, increasing distances that loggers had to travel to work, and worries that the good times might not last.

In the postindustrial period following World War II, the American West itself—now unequivocally industrialized—began to take on the look of permanence, with the Cold War fueling aerospace and weapons production. But the special promise of its once-buoyant natural-resources sectors began to wear thin with the depletion of timber, the end of the Cold War, and an out-migration of people. Competition from producers abroad and the centralizing of processing and manufacturing began to wreak economic and social havoc on many of the region's old mining, agricultural, and lumbering towns. This process of deindustrialization—the disassembling of natural-resource-based economies—has contributed to troubled communities, the persistent and sometimes futile restructuring of local economies, and continued demographic movements in this most transient region in the nation. Beginning with a severe downturn in the Northwest economy in 1980, rural sections of Oregon were important components in that economic makeover.

Structural unemployment, an economist's term for the uprooting of people's lives and other socially disruptive consequences of personal hardship, struck Oregon's timber-dependent districts especially hard in the early 1980s. The rash of mill closures and unemployment reflected a severe slump in the nation's construction trades and a general transformation in the North Pacific Slope's wood-products industry. Those technological and capital shifts included increased mechanization in the woods, the introduction of automated mill equipment, and centralized production in fewer plants. Although Coos Bay may have been the pacesetter in mill closures and high unemployment, the economic malaise quickly spread to other timber districts around the state—mill towns along the Oregon coast, Eugene, Lebanon, and Sweet Home in the Willamette Valley, and to the eastern Oregon communities of Burns and Baker.

The economic troubles were most severe in southern Oregon and in timber counties in the eastern side of the state. The severe recession also reopened the historic divisiveness between rural and urban parts of the state, with Larry Smith, chair of the Baker County Board of Commissioners, declaring: "We're at the wrong end of the stick. We get cracked all the time" (*The Oregonian* 1985). Smith accused Oregon legislators and state agencies of discriminating against rural districts in the distribution of funding. Although the issue of geographic inequity between rural and urban Oregon was an old one, it resurfaced in the early 1980s over lottery money for economic development and support for social programs. Charles Allcock, an economist with Portland General Electric, feared that the growing political and cultural schism between rural and urban Oregon would become a "divisive factor" in state politics (*The Oregonian* 1985). The fact that urban areas in the Willamette Valley fared better than most rural counties further compounded those disparities.

When Portland and the nation emerged relatively unscathed from the economic slump, reporter Julie Tripp reflected that such "comparatively robust recoveries must go down hard" in Oregon's rural counties where unemployment was still on the rise (*The Oregonian* 1985). In December 1984, four of the five counties with the highest unemployment percentages were all timber dependent (Curry, 20.7 percent; Coos, 15.4; Baker, 14.2; and Douglas, 13.7). State employment figures revealed relatively low percentages of unemployment in the state's four major metropolitan areas—Eugene-Springfield, Medford, Portland, and Salem. William Street, a state labor economist in LaGrande, revealed a key characteristic of the new rural economy—a sharp decline in good-paying jobs and an increase in low-wage jobs (*The Oregonian* 1985). In Klamath Falls, new high-tech assembly jobs paid mostly minimum wage, whereas jobs lost in the lumber mills had paid $25,000 to $30,000 a year. U.S. Bancorp's John Mitchell observed that Oregon was undergoing a "major structural change" and predicted that industry would never return to the halcyon days of the 1970s, when the state had enjoyed low interest rates, a rapid rise in population, and sharp increases in construction-related jobs (*The Oregonian* 1985). He also predicted that foreign investors would stay away from rural areas.

Oregon's pioneering land-use planning system, adopted in 1973, became another lightning rod for tensions between rural communities and the Willamette Valley's urban corridor. In the midst of the recession of the early 1980s, opponents of land-use planning launched an initiative effort in 1982 to make the state's land-use authority advisory only. Oregon's leading corporate players—Associated Oregon Industries, Associated General Contractors, Boise Cascade, Georgia-Pacific, and Weyerhaeuser—funded the effort to repeal the planning system. Their initiative was turned back in the fall election when a dying former governor, Tom McCall, issued a dramatic appeal to voters to protect the state's livability and its planning system. The same corporate contributors have bankrolled succeeding efforts to overturn or dramatically alter land-use planning in Oregon. While their campaigns have played to the anxieties of rural voters, their real ambitions have been more self-serving: the development of destination resorts, golf courses, and the conversion of vast forested areas to real-estate enterprises. Developers wanting to extend urban growth boundaries, especially during the state's booming population growth of the 1990s, partnered with those who wanted to repeal land-use planning (Walth 1994, 456-63; Sullivan 1983, 59-60).

"The West as Westerners have known it is changing," the journalist Foster Church observed, and "it will never be the same" (*The Oregonian* 1991). Church was referring to "white flight," the move of middle- and upper-class Californians to sparsely populated rural areas in the West. The Seattle-based *New York Times* correspondent Timothy Egan remarked in 1990 that the old resource towns in the West "have been used up," and the people who lived in those communities were fast becoming an endangered species (Egan 1990). While many of the primary production centers were suffering the ravages of high unemployment and its attendant problems, still others had sprouted boutiques, tanning salons, and luxurious residential areas. The declining fortunes of many rural communities since the early 1980s are obvious: depleted resources, the movement of capital investment to more profitable venues, the consolidation of production, labor-saving technologies, and environmental restrictions. Many people in those communities were and are bitter, finding enemies among environmentalists, well-off urbanites, and the large corporations that had moved on to more lucrative investment opportunities.

While long-time resource towns such as Coos Bay, Roseburg, and Astoria languished with relatively static demographic profiles, below-average wages, and aging populations, others, like Bend and Ashland, have been partner to a new great Western American land rush, with escalating real estate prices, new people, new homes, new wealth, and very different cultural tastes. The new monied classes have introduced social and cultural changes that have been disruptive and unsettling to older residents. Gone are blue-collar jobs in the mills and woods; in their place a new service- and servant-oriented economy has emerged with low-paying, part-time service-sector jobs with no benefits and increasingly unaffordable housing.

Bend and Ashland are "Aspenized" examples of New Western communities that are increasingly layered and polarized as new wealthy classes remake the landscape and social environments of former mining, fishing, and logging towns. Those upscale communities—and others left behind in Oregon's new twenty-first-century economy—reflect opposing sectors of modern capitalism's differentiated landscapes. The swirl of physical, demographic, cultural, and economic change that has taken place in Oregon and the American West during the last one hundred and fifty years provides a striking example of the way modern capitalism has worked its way across the region. If cycles of boom and bust "are as intrinsic to capitalism as earthquakes are to the earth's geology," as the economist Lester Thurow (1996) suggests, then policymakers should expect more of the same in the future. Increasing inequalities in wealth, both within and between rural and urban settings, provide additional evidence of the way modern capitalism produces inequality.[12] With today's dramatically rising unemployment, problematic stock market, dormant national construction industry, and troubles in the state's high-tech sector, Oregon provides a model for Thurow's prediction.

Bibliography

Agnew, John. 1987. *The United States and the World Economy: A Regional Geography*. New York: Cambridge University Press.

Berend, T., and Gyorgy Ranki. 1982. *The European Periphery and Industrialization, 1780-1940*. Cambridge, UK: Cambridge University Press.

Berman, Marshall. 1982. *All That Is Solid Melts into Air: The Experience of Modernity*. New York: Simon & Schuster.

Braudel, Fernand. 1977. *Afterthoughts on Material Civilization and Capitalism*. Trans. Patricia M. Ranum. Baltimore: Johns Hopkins University Press.

Conzen, Michael P. 1977. "The maturing urban system in the United States, 1840-1910." *Annals of the Association of American Geographers* 67 (March).

Cronon, William. 1991. *Nature's Metropolis: Chicago and the Great West*. New York: W. W. Norton.

Danbom, David B. 1995. *Born in the Country: A History of Rural America*. Baltimore: Johns Hopkins University Press.

Dicken, Samuel N., and Emily F. Dicken. 1979. *The Making of Oregon: A Study in Historical Geography*. Portland: Oregon Historical Society Press.

Egan, Timothy. 1990. *The Good Rain: Across Time and Terrain in the Pacific Northwest*. New York: Alfred A. Knopf.

Frazier, Ian. 1989. *Great Plains*. New York: Farrar, Straus & Giroux.

Garreau, Joel. 1981. *The Nine Nations of North America*. Boston: Houghton Mifflin.

Goodwyn, Lawrence. 1978. *The Populist Moment: A Short History of the Agrarian Revolt in America*. New York: Oxford University Press.

Harvey, David. 1985. *The Urbanization of Capital: Studies in the History and Theory of Capitalist Urbanization*. Baltimore: Johns Hopkins University Press.

Hobsbawm, Eric. 1995. *The Age of Extremes: A History of the World, 1914-1991*. New York: Pantheon Books.

Johansen, Dorothy. 1941. *Capitalism on the Far-Western Frontier: The Oregon Steam Navigation Company*. Ph.D. dissertation, University of Washington, Seattle.

Johansen, Dorothy. 1967. *Empire of the Columbia: A History of the Pacific Northwest*. New York: Harper & Row.

Johnston, Robert. 2003. *The Radical Middle Class: Populist Democracy and the Question of Capitalism in Progressive Era Portland*. Princeton: Princeton University Press.

Kennedy, David. 1999. *Freedom from Fear: The American People in Depression and War, 1929-1945*. New York: Oxford University Press.

LaLande, Jeffrey M. 1993. *"It Can't Happen Here" in Oregon: The Jackson County Rebellion, 1932-1933, and its 1890s-1920s Background*. Ph.D. dissertation. University of Oregon, Eugene.

Lipin, Lawrence. 2007. *Workers and the Wild: Conservation, Consumerism, and Labor in Oregon, 1910-30*. Urbana: University of Illinois Press.

MacColl, E. Kimbark. 1988. *Merchants, Money, and Power: The Portland Establishment, 1843-1913*. Portland: The Georgian Press.

McKinley, Charles. 1952. *Uncle Sam in the Pacific Northwest: Federal Management of Natural Resources in the Columbia River Valley*. Berkeley: University of California Press.

Markusen, Ann. 1987. *Regions: The Economics and Politics of Territory*. Totowa, N.J.: Rowan and Littlefield.

McCormick, Thomas J. 1990. "World systems." *Journal of American History* 75 (June): 125-27.

McWilliams, Carey. 1949. *California: The Great Exception*. Santa Barbara, Calif.: Peregrine Smith.

Norris, Kathleen. 1993. *Dakota: A Spiritual Geography*. New York: Ticknor and Fields.

The Oregonian. 1863. Letter from Jesse Applegate to J. W. Nesmith, Nov. 15, 1863, printed Nov. 21, 1863.

The Oregonian. 1865. June 28 edition.

The Oregonian. 1867. July 1 edition.

The Oregonian. 1883. Aug. 14 edition.

The Oregonian. 1888. Jan. 2 edition.

The Oregonian. 1985. Dec. 29 edition.

The Oregonian. 1991. Oct. 20 edition.

Robbins, William G. 1969. *The Far Western Frontier: Economic Opportunity and Social Democracy in Early Roseburg, Oregon*. Ph.D. dissertation. University of Oregon, Eugene.

Robbins, William G. 1994. *Colony and Empire: The Capitalist Transformation of the American West*. Lawrence: University Press of Kansas.

Robbins, William G. 2004. *Landscapes of Conflict: The Oregon Story, 1940-2000*. Seattle: University of Washington Press.

Robbins, William G. 2006. *Hard Times in Paradise: Coos Bay, Oregon, 1850-1986*. Seattle: University of Washington Press.

Roseburg *Plaindealer*. 1873. June 24 and Sept. 29 editions.

Schwantes, Carlos A. 1996. *The Pacific Northwest: An Interpretive History*. Lincoln: University of Nebraska Press.

Salem *Statesman-Journal*. 2008. Aug. 30 edition.

Stavrianos, Leften S. 1976. *The Promise of the Coming Dark Age*. San Francisco: W.H. Freeman.

Sullivan, Edward J. 1983. "The legal evolution of the Oregon planning system," in Abbott, Carl, Deborah Howe, and Sy Adler, eds., *Planning the Oregon Way*. Corvallis: Oregon State University Press.

Thurow, Lester C. 1996. *The Future of Capitalism: How Today's Economic Forces Shape Tomorrow's World*. New York: William Morrow.

Trachtenberg, Alan. 1982. *The Incorporation of America: Culture and Society in the Gilded Age*. New York: Hill and Wang.

U.S. Bureau of the Census. 1940. *Sixteenth Census of the United States, 1940: Vol. 1, Population, Number of Inhabitants*. U.S. Washington, D.C.: U.S. Bureau of the Census.

U.S. Bureau of the Census. 1950. *Seventeenth Census of the United States: Census of Population, 1950: Vol. 2, Characteristics of the Population*. Washington, D.C.: U.S. Bureau of the Census.

Walth, Brent. 1994. *Fire at Eden's Gate: Tom McCall and the Oregon Story*. Portland: Oregon Historical Society Press.

Watkins, Marilyn. 1995. *Rural Democracy: Family Farmers and Politics in Western Washington, 1890-1925*. Ithaca, N.Y.: Cornell University Press.

West Shore. 1875. Vol. 1, no. 1, August edition.

Winther, Oscar O. 1950. *Old Oregon Country: A History of Frontier Trade, Transportation, and Travel*. Palo Alto, Calif.: Stanford University Press.

Wood, Richard E. 2008. *Survival of Rural America: Small Victories and Bitter Harvests*. Lawrence: University Press of Kansas.

Chapter 5

The Declining Economic Interdependence of the Portland Metropolitan Core and Its Periphery

David Holland
Paul Lewin
Bruce Sorte
Bruce Weber

Introduction

For many decades, rural areas in many parts of the United States, including the Pacific Northwest, have lagged economically behind urban centers. Nonetheless, rural and urban economies haven't developed separately. In fact, some have suggested that urban economic vitality ought to be viewed as a resource for rural areas, and that rural policy ought to pursue a strategy of strengthening rural-urban economic linkages (Porter et al. 2004; Stauber 2001). Not very much is known, however, about the economic relationship between urban centers and their rural hinterlands.

Better understanding of these economic linkages would aid policymakers as they seek new and more robust strategies for increasing rural economic well-being (Harrison and Sieb 1990). At the same time, a clearer sense of how rural and urban economies work together could generate new policy and investments that provide urban residents with a broader set of options for meeting their own economic needs and generally improving their quality of life.

Holland et al. (1992) used 1982 data to study employment and trade interactions between the Portland metro area (referred to as the economic "core") and its surrounding trade area (referred to by economic geographers as the "periphery"). Their objective was to determine the significance of the economic output of both the Portland urban core and surrounding rural periphery for meeting each other's demand for goods and services. In addition, they investigated the interdependence of urban and rural labor markets, the most important sectors in core-periphery trade, and the relative importance of households and businesses in generating demand in each subregion for products and services from the other. This chapter reexamines this economic linkage in light of recent data and investigates how the economic interdependence of the Portland metro core and its relatively rural periphery trade area has changed from 1982 to 2006.

Economic Regions and Central-Place Theory: A Way of Thinking about Interdependent Urban and Rural Economies

The core-periphery model has its roots in what economic geographers have termed "central-place theory" (Christaller 1966). This way of describing economic regions (such as the Willamette Valley, the Columbia River basin, and even the state of Oregon) suggests that there is an ordering of cities within a region. Such an ordering begins with the more rural hamlets, villages, and towns that, by definition, are places where the economic activity is more local and more service oriented.

At the upper end of the ordering are regional cities, primary cities where all goods and services, including higher-order services such as medical and financial services, are available. When people living in smaller (lower-order) towns and villages need some of these services, they must travel to primary cities to obtain them. Of course, many important goods and services (for example, agricultural products, lumber and wood, oil, coal, and fish) are necessarily produced in the periphery and tend to flow up and through the primary cities to the rest of the world. The basic idea of central-place theory is that small towns are not just scaled-down primary cities but must be viewed in relationship to primary cities in their economic region to better understand all the economic forces at play. Viewed from this perspective, both the Portland metro area and its surrounding rural communities are part of a unified economic region, with each portion of that region playing an important and unique role.

The Bureau of Economic Analysis of the U.S. Department of Commerce has mapped the principal trading regions of the United States into economic areas (U.S. Department of Commerce 1975), groups of counties that constitute functional economic regions according to the central-place perspective. For purposes of economic development it is strategically useful, for both primary cities in the core and rural communities in the periphery, to define economic regions using the logic of central-place theory.

Urban and Rural: How Are They Linked Economically?

Dabson (2007) identifies important rural contributions to metro prosperity and metro contributions to rural prosperity. Rural areas provide market goods and services that tend to require extensive land and/or particular natural resources, as well as nonmarket services such as ecosystem services and recreational experiences, and educated workers. Metro areas, in turn, provide markets, critical specialized services, jobs for those leaving rural areas for better opportunity, and financial resources that support many of the public and private investments in rural people and places.

Are rural and urban areas really economically interdependent? In a global sense, as Dabson points out, the answer is certainly yes. In the case of a major central place such as Portland, however, the interdependence of core and periphery in both labor markets and trade does not include all the links Dabson identifies. For most industries in both regions, the bulk of trade takes place outside the functional economic region; that is, with the rest of the world. Most agricultural production and forest production in the periphery of the Portland trade area, for example, is shipped out of the region rather than to the Portland core. Yet the health of the rural economy and rural demand for Portland metro goods and services are important for businesses in such major urban sectors as wholesale and retail trade, financial services, and consumer services—in which the majority of Portland-core export sales are made to the rural periphery—as well as to rural-area quality of life. In addition, where there are important trade linkages from periphery to core, such as Portland's processing of agricultural commodities, core industries have an interest in the economic health of the periphery. Food-packing plants in Portland need a steady supply of fruits and vegetables from the surrounding rural areas. If raw materials become unavailable or unaffordable, a plant might have to shut its doors. Even in this extreme example, however, the economic impact of raw-material shortages from the periphery would be likely to stop at the processor level, rather than cascading through the economy.

To take a real-life example, timber-harvest restrictions in the western Oregon periphery have been linked to reduced sales for Portland core businesses. Waters et al. (1994) found that about 15 percent of the total regional economic impact of timber-supply shocks would be felt in Portland, with most of this impact coming from reduced household spending in the periphery for core-produced services, rather than from reduced output of wood products in Portland.

Rural demand for goods and services can also affect the urban core. Simply put, declines in rural household and business income will be felt as declining demand for Portland-based services. Given the central-place nature of these services, it is likely that there will be limited alternative demand for them outside the Portland functional economic region. A periphery in economic decline will place a drag on the service economy in the urban subregion. That said, a major downturn in the economy of the periphery would be felt in the urban center, but it would have to be substantial to produce a large effect. For instance, an analysis of the effects of the policy to reduce federal timber harvest after the 1990 listing of the northern spotted owl as a threatened species under the Endangered Species Act—by most accounts a substantial shock to rural timber communities—revealed that the reduced timber harvest in the western Oregon periphery caused an estimated loss of 4,400 jobs in Portland, or 0.8 percent of the total (Waters et al. 1994).

The urban-development literature does not generally consider the interdependence of urban and rural areas (see Berube 2007 for a good example). Those writing about the development of rural places, however, will typically address the importance of connections between urban and rural areas. Porter et al. (2004, 60), for example, have suggested a need for a "holistic policy framework" for rural economic development that "incorporate[s] linkages between the rural region and nearby urban areas." In the literature on rural economic development, "there is a growing understanding that the central issue is competitiveness, and there is widespread agreement on the importance of cluster thinking." Chapter 8 discusses clusters in the Portland trade area that link the rural periphery and metro core and have potential for strengthening the economies of both.

Labor and Earnings Flow

The Portland, Oregon, trade area that we examine in this chapter includes all of western Oregon and parts of central Oregon and southwest Washington.

We define the Portland trade area to include both the Portland Economic Area and the Eugene Economic Area as defined for 1982 by the Bureau of Economic Analysis of the U.S. Department of Commerce.[1] The trade area has as its economic center a metropolitan core, which we define as the four counties in the 1982 Standard Metropolitan Statistical Area: Multnomah, Washington, and Clackamas counties in Oregon and Clark County in Washington. For the remainder of this chapter, we will use "Portland" as a shorthand reference to this metropolitan area definition. The trade-area periphery of the Portland metro core consists of Benton, Clatsop, Columbia, Coos, Crook, Curry, Deschutes, Douglas, Hood River, Jackson, Jefferson, Josephine, Klamath, Lake, Lane, Lincoln, Linn, Marion, Polk, Sherman, Tillamook, Wasco, and Yamhill counties in Oregon and Cowlitz, Klickitat, Skamania, and Wahkiakum counties in Washington.

The Portland trade area is bounded on the north by the Seattle trade area, which extends into southwestern Washington, and extends south to the California border. The western boundary is defined by the Pacific Ocean and the eastern boundary extends to the Boise trade area, which dominates eastern Oregon.

Although Portland's core and its periphery are not strongly linked through flows of labor and income, we see that they have over time become more interdependent through commuting.

We calculated labor flows—the movement of workers back and forth between Portland and its periphery—for both 1980 and 2000 from census information (U.S. Department of Commerce, Bureau of the Census 1980 and 2008) and constructed earnings flows with data from the Bureau of Economic Analysis (U.S. Department of Commerce, Bureau of Economic Analysis 1988 and 2008). A detailed explanation of our estimation procedures and assumptions may be found in Holland et al. (2009).

Holland et al.'s (1993) estimates of labor and earnings flows for 1982 are shown in table 1, with earnings reported in inflation-adjusted 2006 dollars. Each earnings flow appears below the corresponding labor flow. Reading across the rows, we can see, for example, how many of the 568,916 workers who lived in the core in 1980 worked in the core, how many worked in the periphery, and how many worked outside the core-periphery region. We also can see how much of the approximately $18 billion in labor earnings that originated in the core in 1982 stayed in the core and how much left for the periphery or for outside the core-periphery region in the pockets of workers

Place of Residence (P. o. R.)	Flows	Place of Work (P. o. W.)				
		Core	Periphery	Elsewhere	Total jobs* by P.o.R.	Total earnings by P.o.R.
Core	Jobs	555,857	8,434	4,625	568,916	
	$ Earnings	17,921,323	345,977	171,109		18,438,409
Periphery	Jobs	15,917	547,431	33,013	596,361	
	$ Earnings	340,857	14,915,804	668,417		15,925,078
Elsewhere	Jobs	14,300	5,949			
	$ Earnings	403,884	213,782			
Total Jobs by P.o.W.		586,074	561,814			
Total $ Earnings by P.o.W.		18,666,064	15,475,562			

Table 1. Labor and earnings flows between the core and the periphery, 1982 (thousands of 2006 dollars). Note: Includes both full- and part-time jobs. Sources: Holland et al. (1993); U.S. Department of Commerce, Bureau of the Census (1980); U.S. Department of Commerce, Bureau of Economic Analysis (1988).

Place of Residence (P. o. R.)	Flows	Place of Work (P. o. W.)				
		Core	Periphery	Elsewhere	Total jobs* by P.o.R.	Total earnings by P.o.R.
Core	Jobs	866,761	18,575	7,839	893,175	
	$ Earnings	50,287,477	888,001	575,514		51,750,992
Periphery	Jobs	44,932	793,472	9,166	847,570	
	$ Earnings	2,368,396	34,463,113	464,318		37,295,827
Elsewhere	Jobs	6,151	5,949			
	$ Earnings	281,640	224,448			
Total Jobs by P.o.W.		917,844	817,996			
Total $ Earnings by P.o.W.		52,937,512	35,575,563			

Table 2. Labor and earnings flows between the core and the periphery, 2006 (thousands of dollars). Note: Includes both full- and part-time jobs. Sources: U.S. Department of Commerce, Bureau of Economic Analysis (undated); U.S. Department of Commerce, Bureau of the Census (2008).

who lived outside the core. Likewise, reading down the columns, we can see where the workers who commuted into the core and periphery lived.

Our estimates of labor and earnings flows between core and periphery for 2006 are shown in tables 2 and 3. The number of periphery-to-Portland-core commuters roughly tripled from 1982 to 2006; the number of Portland-core-to-periphery commuters also increased over this period, though not nearly as quickly.

Place of Residence	Flows	Place of Work			
		1982		2006	
		Core	Periphery	Core	Periphery
Core	Jobs	94.8%	1.5%	94.4%	2.3%
	Earnings	96.0%	2.2%	95.0%	2.5%
Periphery	Jobs	2.7%	97.4%	4.9%	97.0%
	Earnings	1.8%	96.4%	4.5%	96.9%
Elsewhere	Jobs	2.4%	1.1%	0.7%	0.7%
	Earnings	2.2%	1.4%	0.5%	0.6%
Total Jobs by Place of Work		100.0%	100.0%	100.0%	100.0%
Total Earnings by Place of Work		100.0%	100.0%	100.0%	100.0%

Table 3. Percentage of core and periphery jobs and earnings going to residents of each region, 1982 and 2006.

Interregional Trade in Goods and Services

Trade in goods and services is a much more significant linkage between core and periphery than is commuting. We used regional commodity reports from a model of economic exchanges between Portland core counties and periphery counties (IMPLAN) to estimate trade in goods and services between the core and its periphery trade area, and between the combined core-periphery area and the rest of the United States, based on a procedure developed by Holland and Pirnique (2000). A detailed account of the estimation procedures may be found in Holland et al. (2009).

Trade between core and periphery

In 1982, the economies of the core and the periphery were roughly equal in terms of size, as measured by total sales (table 4). The Portland core economy exported 37 percent of its production[2]—a sign that its economy was relatively open to both its periphery and the rest of the world. There was significant trade with the surrounding region: 20 percent of Portland's exports went to its trade-area periphery communities and consumers. The core imported slightly more goods and services than it exported, but the net trade balance between Portland and its trade-area periphery was positive and large, with the value of Portland's exports of goods and services to its periphery ($4.5 billion in 2006 dollars) more than twice the value of its imports from the periphery ($1.9 billion).

The economy of the periphery was similar, exporting 38 percent of production and importing 44 percent of the periphery's goods and services, but

From	To core	To periphery	To rest of world	Total sales
Core Total	36,562	**4,473**	**17,533**	58,567
Core Goods	7,486	1,321	10,492	19,299
Core Services	29,076	3,151	7,041	39,268
Periphery Total	1,936	37,326	**21,407**	60,669
Periphery Goods	1,396	10,898	19,003	31,297
Periphery Services	540	26,428	2,404	29,372
Rest of World Total	**21,083**	**25,060**		
Rest of World Goods	14,256	16,694		
Rest of World Services	6,826	8,366		
Total Purchases	59,581	66,858		
Total Goods Purchases	23,138	28,914		
Total Services Purchases	36,442	37,944		

Table 4. Portland core-periphery goods and services trade, 1982 (millions of dollars). Source: Holland et al. 1993, from IMPLAN data.

only 8 percent of the periphery's exports went to the Portland metropolitan area core. More than $2.5 billion flowed from the periphery to Portland on the trade account, most of it in the service sector (table 4).

Between 1982 and 2006, output grew in both core and periphery, but the core's growth was much faster. Core exports to the periphery grew by over 60 percent, while periphery exports to the core actually declined. Because of these changes, the Portland core's overall (goods and services) trade surplus with the periphery was more than $5 billion in 2006, double its 1982 value. Most of the trade surplus was generated in the service sectors, with service exports from core to periphery of $5.53 billion and imports of services to the core from the periphery of $855 million (table 5).

When core-periphery trade is viewed in relative terms, however, we see that the trade linkages have declined over time. In 1982 the core was exporting roughly 8 percent of its output to the periphery. By 2006, exports to the periphery represented only 4 percent of this output. The relative importance of core-periphery trade declined in part because, over the same interval, the core's exports to the rest of the world grew dramatically: the proportion of goods and services exported from the core to the rest of the world increased from 30 to 35 percent.

Periphery-core trade also declined both absolutely and relatively, in part because intra-periphery trade grew rapidly. In 1982 the periphery was ex-

From		Core	Periphery	Rest of world	Total sales
Core	Total	115,271	**7,402**	65,044	187,716
	Goods	19,610	**1,869**	40,667	62,146
	Services	95,661	**5,533**	24,377	125,570
Periphery	Total	**1,816**	81,874	36,331	120,022
	Goods	**961**	14,372	25,379	40,712
	Services	**855**	67,503	10,952	79,310
Rest of world	Total	61,712	46,900		
	Goods	36,191	31,116		
	Services	25,521	15,784		
Total purchases	Total	178,799	136,176		
	Goods	56,762	47,357		
	Services	122,037	88,820		

(The "To" spans the Core, Periphery, Rest of world, and Total sales columns.)

Table 5. Portland core-periphery goods and services trade, 2006 (millions of dollars). Source: Authors' calculations from 2006 IMPLAN data.

porting 3 percent of its goods and services to the core; by 2006, the figure was only 2 percent. As economic activity has diversified and become more geographically dispersed in the last quarter-century, some specialized goods and services that were once available only in large cities, such as specialized medical and business services, have become available in the periphery. The result has been a relative weakening in the trade linkages between the Portland core and its periphery as the periphery has become more self-sufficient. Goods and services both produced and consumed in the periphery increased from 62 percent of output in 1982 to 68 percent of output in 2006.

Trade with rest of the world

A comparison of tables 4 and 5 shows that the Portland core's rate of economic growth was about twice that of the periphery. This growth was led by the expansion of goods exports from the core to the rest of the world and coincides with the emergence of both microprocessors and sports apparel as signature Portland industries. In fact, the Portland core's export of goods grew faster than its export of services at a time when service sectors nationally were increasing faster than good-producing sectors.

Goods exports from the core to the rest of the world were growing at four times the rate of goods exports from the periphery. By 2006, the Portland core had transformed itself into an export-driven economy with a positive trade balance, something that was not the case in 1982. The periphery, on the other hand, with its mix of resource-based goods, was less successful in expanding its exports and remained a regional economy with a negative trade balance (tables 4 and 5).

Changing Relationships

Over the past quarter-century, the Portland trade area has grown rapidly and has experienced significant changes in industrial structure and in the relationship between its core economy and that of the periphery. In the period between our two studies, decreasing transportation costs and improved communication technology have enabled regional economies to expand export sales to more-distant markets. Likewise, increased imports from more-distant places have become available and have expanded.

At the same time, these forces have encouraged the decentralization of some parts of the marketing and service sector; some firms or functions that were once at home only in the core have migrated into the periphery. Regional centers in the periphery have taken over medical procedures as well as retail and wholesale functions that formerly were conducted in the core. The result has been a weakening of the central-place hierarchy as a description of economic organization over the economic area investigated here.

To better understand this change in relationships, we developed a detailed input-output model for the economy of core and periphery in this economic area. An input-output model organizes information about trade between regional firms and households and those outside the region, making it possible to analyze the ways in which changes in industry composition, exports, and consumption patterns or habits in one subregion affect businesses and households in the other. Our analysis for this economic area over the period from 1982 to 2006 (see Appendix that follows for technical details) points to five major conclusions about rural-urban economic interdependence in the region:

- The core has grown faster than the periphery, mainly because of rapid growth in goods exports.
- Commuting flows between the core and periphery have increased.
- Commuting linkages have grown stronger as the core has grown, both in numbers of commuters and also relative to the size of the respective labor

forces. At the same time, both core and periphery represent relatively self-contained labor markets. In 1980, only 1.5 percent of the resident Portland core labor force worked in the periphery, while roughly 2.7 percent of periphery residents worked in Portland. By 2000, 2.1 percent of the Portland core resident workforce worked in the periphery, and 5.3 of the periphery resident workforce worked in the Portland core.

- Core-periphery trade flows have weakened as the core has expanded trade to other regions and as the periphery has become more self-contained.
- Spillover impacts of exports (the cross-regional effect of exports from one subregion on sales in the other) have generally weakened in both core and periphery, although at a much greater rate in the core.[3] Even with the absolute declines in linkage strength since 1982, a given change in economic activity (for better or worse) in the periphery still affects the core more than such a change in the core affects the periphery. The city, in sum, is more sensitive to changes in the rural economy than the rural areas are to changes in the city's economy.

Both core and periphery still have a significant interest in each other's economic health: 18 percent of the indirect and induced impact of a shock to the periphery economy leaks across to the core economy, and 7 percent of indirect and induced impact of a shock to the core economy spills over to the periphery.

Conclusion

As the larger Portland trade area has grown over the past quarter-century, the core economy has grown faster than the periphery. Slightly smaller than that of the periphery in 1982, the core economy was 50 percent larger in 2006, a stunning rate of change. The Portland core depends increasingly (though modestly) on the periphery as a source of labor, but it depends on it less than in previous decades as a market for its goods and services. The periphery, in turn, increasingly depends on the Portland core as a source of personal income for its residents, and has continued to purchase needed goods and services from the core while increasing its local production. The periphery depends less on Portland as a market for its goods and services than it did in previous decades.

Yet the fortunes of each region are still affected by growth or decline in the other. Growth in exports from the periphery has a significant cross-regional impact on the Portland core: about one-sixth of the indirect and induced economic impact of periphery exports accrues to the Portland core.[4] The Portland core benefits more from a given level of growth in periphery exports than the periphery benefits from the same level of growth in core exports. Nonetheless, given the size and growth of the Portland core economy, Portland core exports have a significant impact on the periphery. Each region benefits from growth in the other subregion's economy and is harmed by decline. The futures of the core and the periphery in the Portland trade area are inextricably intertwined.

Appendix: The Multi-Regional Input-Output (MRIO) Model
Model closure

To estimate the impacts of economic activity in one place on economic activity in another, economists have developed multi-regional input-output (MRIO) models that allow an analyst to estimate "spillovers" showing how changes in exports from a core urban region affect production of goods and services in the surrounding periphery. To understand economic interdependence and model these spillovers for Oregon, we developed a MRIO model of the Portland core and western Oregon periphery.

In creating the model, we treated household income and expenditures in the two-region area as "endogenous," meaning that the spending of this income has the effect of increasing regional demand and output in the part of the economic region where it is spent. We identified nine distinct household income classes for the Portland core and periphery from IMPLAN data. IMPLAN is a commercially available database and software that can be used to construct input-output models for any county or combination of counties in the United States. The model identifies linkages across regions according to industry, factor of production, and household income class. Thus the model is able to show how a shock to the periphery economy—for example, a mill shutdown—affects industry output and household income in the periphery region and in the core.

The model assumes that regional consumption for each household income class is a function of the personal income received by that household group: households spend what they earn. Personal income is the sum of employee compensation, proprietors' income, government transfers, and property income. The regional contribution to regional personal income is measured as the sum of employee compensation and proprietors' income from the IM-

PLAN input-output accounts. All "other property income" generated in the region is assumed to be paid to capital owners outside the combined region. Payments of interest, dividends, and rent to households and government transfers in each region were treated as exogenous and were derived from the IMPLAN Social Accounting Matrix (SAM) constructed for each region.

Each industry is assumed to pay a fixed proportion of earnings to commuting workers from each region and the proportion is assumed to be constant for all industries in the region. As is conventional in SAM-type models, employee compensation and proprietors' income are assumed to be distributed in fixed but different proportions across the size distribution of households in each region. The marginal propensity to consume is assumed to be equal to the average propensity to consume for each household income class. As is true for the standard input-output analysis, this model is static and reflects conditions at a moment in time, not changes occurring over an extended period and affected by multiple "shocks" or economic challenges.

Output multipliers

Household-endogenous output multipliers are derived from the Leontief inverse matrix of the multiregional transactions table. The own-region output multipliers are the column sums of inter-industry coefficients in the diagonal blocks of this matrix. These multipliers capture both inter-industry linkages within the region and feedback effects from changes in activity in the other region induced by a shock in the first region. The cross-regional multipliers are the column sums of inter-industry coefficients in the off-diagonal blocks of the inverse matrix. They show the output change across regions for a one-unit change in the exogenous demand of the opposite region.

Own- and cross-regional output multipliers for the Portland core and the trade-area periphery are shown in table 6. The own-region effect in 2006 of a $1 increase in crop exports in the periphery, for example, is a $1.59 increase in total output in the periphery economy. Simultaneously, because the cross-regional multiplier for the core is 0.12, this would result in a $0.12 increase in total output in the core. The sum of the own-region and cross-region effects yields the total effect of the increase in exports on the entire trade-area economy. Thus, in our example, a $1 increase in periphery crop exports would generate a $1.71 increase in output in the trade area.

The range of core-to-periphery cross-regional output multipliers for 2006 (excluding household industry) is between 0.03 (for forest products and log-

Sector	1982						2006					
	Core			Periphery			Core			Periphery		
	Core	Periphery	Total	Periphery	Core	Total	Core	Periphery	Total	Periphery	Core	Total
Crops	1.82	0.13	1.95	1.63	0.18	1.81	1.57	0.04	1.61	1.59	0.12	1.71
Livestock	1.65	0.13	1.78	1.77	0.18	1.95	1.65	0.09	1.75	1.90	0.17	2.07
Forest Products & Logging	1.78	0.18	1.96	1.84	0.14	1.98	1.78	0.03	1.80	1.91	0.20	2.11
Commercial Fishing	1.53	0.06	1.59	1.37	0.13	1.50	1.81	0.04	1.85	1.89	0.18	2.07
Landscaping & Ag. Services	1.75	0.11	1.86	1.60	0.18	1.78	1.81	0.06	1.87	1.79	0.15	1.94
Mining	1.58	0.08	1.66	1.48	0.14	1.62	2.04	0.06	2.09	1.58	0.17	1.75
Construction	1.80	0.08	1.88	1.60	0.20	1.80	1.76	0.06	1.82	1.70	0.14	1.83
Other Manufacturing	1.60	0.08	1.68	1.50	0.19	1.69	1.78	0.09	1.87	1.86	0.22	2.08
Food Processing	1.69	0.19	1.88	1.79	0.25	2.04	1.71	0.04	1.75	1.56	0.15	1.71
Wood Products	2.12	0.25	2.37	2.18	0.21	2.39	1.88	0.06	1.94	1.87	0.19	2.06
Pulp & Paper Products	1.69	0.13	1.82	1.66	0.19	1.85	1.65	0.04	1.69	1.68	0.19	1.87
Electronics & Instruments	1.68	0.07	1.75	1.55	0.20	1.75	2.01	0.05	2.06	1.75	0.21	1.97
Transportation	1.94	0.07	2.01	1.58	0.18	1.76	1.76	0.05	1.81	1.74	0.14	1.88
Communications	1.46	0.05	1.51	1.41	0.12	1.53	1.78	0.04	1.82	1.73	0.14	1.88
Utilities	1.61	0.21	1.82	1.32	0.08	1.40	1.72	0.04	1.76	1.51	0.17	1.68
Wholesale Trade	1.72	0.08	1.80	1.59	0.19	1.78	1.69	0.05	1.74	1.67	0.14	1.81
Retail Trade	1.67	0.07	1.74	1.57	0.17	1.74	1.71	0.05	1.76	1.70	0.13	1.83
Financial	1.80	0.07	1.87	1.61	0.19	1.80	1.78	0.05	1.83	1.76	0.12	1.89
Insurance & Real Estate	1.42	0.03	1.45	1.23	0.06	1.29	1.67	0.04	1.71	1.62	0.11	1.73
Eating, Drinking & Lodging	1.79	0.11	1.90	1.63	0.22	1.85	1.73	0.07	1.79	1.75	0.16	1.92
Other Services	1.67	0.07	1.74	1.54	0.16	1.70	1.82	0.05	1.87	1.79	0.15	1.94
Business Services	1.72	0.07	1.79	1.60	0.18	1.78	1.84	0.06	1.90	1.83	0.16	1.99
Health Services	1.84	0.08	1.92	1.69	0.19	1.88	1.78	0.06	1.84	1.76	0.14	1.91
Govt. Industry & Enterprise	1.74	0.09	1.83	1.64	0.18	1.82	1.74	0.07	1.81	1.75	0.14	1.89
Household Industry & Other	1.05	0.01	1.06	1.05	0.01	1.06	1.37	0.02	1.38	1.42	0.07	1.48

Table 6. Own-region and cross-region multipliers for Portland trade area core and periphery, 1982 and 2006.

ging) and 0.09 (for other manufacturing) (table 6). The magnitude of the cross-regional output multiplier is a rough indication of that sector's backward linkage (input purchases) with the other region's economy.

The cross-regional output effects, and thus the economic linkages, from the periphery to the Portland core generally are stronger than the linkages in the opposite direction (table 6). The largest multipliers from periphery to core are in the other manufacturing and forest products/logging sectors. The range of cross-regional output multipliers (excluding household industry) is between 0.11 (for insurance and real estate) and 0.22 (for other manufacturing). As a general rule, unit changes in final demand for periphery goods and services generate output changes ranging from 0.15 to 0.20 in the Portland core economy. The periphery-to-core cross-regional output multipliers are uniformly two or more times larger than the corresponding core-to-periphery multipliers, indicating that backward linkages from periphery to core are generally stronger than those from core to periphery.

The cross-regional multipliers from the core to the periphery were almost all considerably smaller in 2006 than they were in 1982 (table 6). This reflects a general weakening of core imports from the periphery relative to the size of the core economy. In contrast, the cross-regional multipliers from the periphery to the core are, for many industries, larger in 2006 than they were in 1982, reflecting a relative strengthening of periphery imports from the core.

In contrast to the core, where many own-region multipliers declined from 1982 to 2006, many of the periphery own-region multipliers increased over this time period. This was especially true for the periphery's service industries, for which virtually all multipliers increased over the time period (table 6).This probably indicates import substitution on the part of many periphery industries, as formerly imported goods and services have been replaced by those produced by firms in the periphery.

Spillover coefficients

In a core-periphery input-output model, the spillover coefficient shows what portion of total indirect and induced effect occurs in the opposite region. For example, the spillover coefficient for the livestock sector in the metro region in 1982 is 0.17 (table 7). This means that 17 cents of every dollar of indirect and induced effect associated with core livestock exports spills over into the periphery region. The spillover coefficient measures the strength of cross regional impact associated with expansion or contraction of an own-region

Sector	1982		2006	
	Core	Periphery	Core	Periphery
Crops	0.14	0.22	0.07	0.17
Livestock	0.17	0.19	0.12	0.16
Forest Products & Logging	0.19	0.14	0.04	0.18
Commercial Fishing	0.10	0.26	0.05	0.17
Landscaping & Ag. Services	0.13	0.23	0.07	0.16
Mining	0.12	0.23	0.06	0.23
Construction	0.09	0.25	0.07	0.17
Other Manufacturing	0.12	0.28	0.10	0.20
Food Processing	0.22	0.24	0.05	0.21
Wood Products	0.18	0.15	0.06	0.18
Pulp & Paper Products	0.16	0.22	0.06	0.22
Electronics & Instruments	0.09	0.27	0.05	0.22
Transportation	0.07	0.24	0.06	0.16
Communications	0.10	0.23	0.05	0.16
Utilities	0.26	0.20	0.05	0.25
Wholesale Trade	0.10	0.24	0.07	0.17
Retail Trade	0.09	0.23	0.07	0.16
Financial	0.08	0.24	0.06	0.13
Insurance & Real Estate	0.07	0.21	0.06	0.15
Eating, Drinking & Lodging	0.12	0.26	0.09	0.17
Other Services	0.09	0.23	0.06	0.16
Business Services	0.09	0.23	0.07	0.16
Health Services	0.09	0.22	0.07	0.15
Govt. Industry & Enterprise	0.11	0.22	0.09	0.16
Household Industry & Other	0.17	0.17	0.05	0.15
Average Spillover Coefficient	0.13	0.22	0.07	0.18

Table 7. Spillover coefficients for Portland trade-area core and periphery, 1982 and 2006.

sector. It is calculated as the cross-regional multiplier for each sector (e.g., 0.13 for 1982 core livestock sector; table 6) divided by the total periphery livestock multiplier from table 8 minus one (1.78-1 = 0.78). So the spillover coefficient is 0.17 (0.13/0.78).

The average (unweighted) spillover coefficient in 1982 was much larger for the periphery than for the core: 22 percent of the total regional (core plus periphery) indirect and induced effects of exports from the periphery spilled over to the core compared with only 13 percent in the other direction.

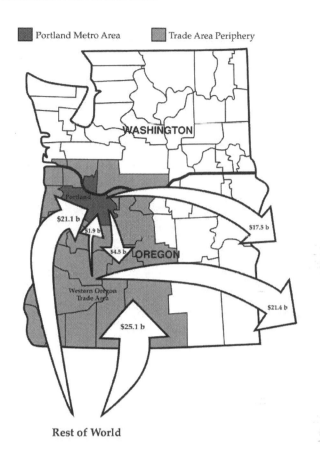

Figure 1. Trade flows, Portland core and trade-area periphery, 1982 (billions of current dollars).

The metro sectors with the largest spillover coefficients in 1982 were food processing and utilities (table 7) because these sectors purchased important production inputs from the periphery economy. More than 20 percent of the indirect and induced economic impact of every dollar of exports from the core for these two industries was felt in the periphery. However, the spillover coefficients of the rapidly expanding metro service and electronic industries in the core were less than 10 percent, indicating that very little of the economic impact from expansion in these sectors spilled over into the periphery. In 1982 most periphery sectors exhibited spillover coefficients greater than 20 percent (table 7, figure 1). For many periphery sectors, most of this effect is in the form of induced rural household spending for Portland-produced services.

Between 1982 and 2006, the average spillover effect of exports declined in both core and periphery (figure 2); changes in each region generally have

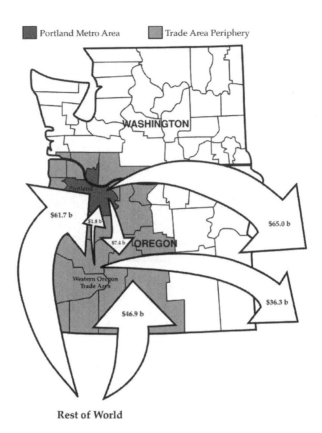

Figure 2. Trade flows, Portland core and trade-area periphery, 2006 (billions of current dollars).

less impact on the other than they did in the early 1980s. The average core-to-periphery spillover effect declined by over 45 percent, from 0.13 to 0.07, while the average periphery-to-core spillover declined by less than 20 percent, from 0.22 to 0.18. For several natural-resource sectors and utilities, the periphery-to-core spillover effects increased between 1982 and 2006: for logging the spillover coefficient increased from 0.14 to 0.18; for wood products, from 0.15 to 0.18; and for utilities, from 0.20 to 0.25. For all other periphery sectors, the spillovers declined or stayed the same. Core-to-periphery spillover effects declined in all sectors, and in the case of natural-resource industries and utilities the decline was significant. For logging, for example, the spillover coefficient declined from 0.19 in 1982 to 0.04 in 2006. Wood products declined from 0.18 to 0.06, and pulp and paper declined from 0.16 to 0.06. Utilities declined from 0.26 to 0.05.

Bibliography

Berube, Alan. 2007. *Metronation: How U.S. Metropolitan Areas Fuel American Prosperity.* Washington, D.C.: The Brookings Institution.

Christaller, W. 1966. *Central Places in Southern Germany.* Transl. C. W. Baskin. Englewood Cliffs, N.J.: Prentice Hall.

Dabson, Brian. 2007. "Rural-urban interdependence: Why metropolitan and rural America need each other." Background paper prepared for the Blueprint for American Prosperity, November 2007. Washington, D.C.: The Brookings Institution. http://www.brookings.edu/projects/blueprint.aspx. Consulted June 4, 2009.

Harrison, David, and Jonathan Sieb. 1990. "Toward one region: Strengthening rural-urban economic linkages." *Northwest Report* 9: 1-12 (April 1990); published by Northwest Area Foundation, St. Paul, Minn.

Holland, D., and F. Pirnique. 2000. *Some Procedures for Estimating Goods and Service Trade Between Regions Using Trade Data from IMPLAN.* Agricultural Economics Staff Paper A.E. 2000-3. Department of Agricultural Economics, Washington State University, Pullman.

Holland, D., B. Weber, and E. Waters. 1992. *Modeling the Economic Linkage Between Core and Periphery Regions: The Portland, Oregon Trade Area.* Working Paper No. 92-103, August 1992. Corvallis: Department of Agricultural and Resource Economics, Oregon State University.

Holland, D., B. Weber, and E. Waters. 1993. *How Interdependent Are Rural and Urban Areas?* Staff Paper No. 93-6, March 1993. Department of Agricultural Economics, Washington State University, Pullman.

Holland, D., P. Lewin, B. Sorte, and B. Weber. 2009. *How Economically Interdependent Is the Portland Metro Core with Its Rural Periphery? A Comparison across Two Decades.* Working Paper RSP 09-01, February 2009. Corvallis: Rural Studies Program, Oregon State University.

Porter, Michael E., C. Ketels, K. Miller, and R. T. Bryden. 2004. *Competitiveness in Rural U.S. Regions: Learning and Research Agenda.* February 25, 2004. Cambridge, Mass.: Harvard Business School.

Stauber, Karl N. 2001. "Why invest in rural America—and how? A critical public policy question for the 21st century." *Economic Review* (Federal Reserve Bank of Kansas City), 2nd quarter, 33-63.

U.S. Department of Commerce, Bureau of the Census. 1980. 1980 Census of Population Journey to Work STF4 Documentation, Supplement 1 Tabulation P-B34. Place of Work Destinations. Washington, D.C.: U.S. Department of Commerce.

U.S. Department of Commerce, Bureau of the Census. 2008. *United States Census 2000, County-To-County Worker Flow Files.* http://www.census.gov/population/www.cen2000/commuting/index.html. Accessed March 29, 2009.

U.S. Department of Commerce, Bureau of Economic Analysis, Regional Economic Analysis Division. 1975. "The BEA economic areas: structural changes and growth, 1950-73." Survey of Current Business 55(11): 14-25. Washington, D.C.: U.S. Department of Commerce.

U.S. Department of Commerce, Bureau of Economic Analysis. 1988. Local Area Personal Income 1981-86, Vol. 5: Southwest, Rocky Mountain and Far West Regions, and Alaska and Hawaii. Washington, D.C.: U.S. Department of Commerce.

U.S. Department of Commerce, Bureau of Economic Analysis. (undated). "Regional economics accounts, personal income and employment summary." http://www.bea.gov/regional/reis/default.cfm?catable+CA04.

Waters, E. C., D. W. Holland, and B. A. Weber. 1994. "Interregional effects of reduced timber harvests: The impact of the Northern Spotted Owl." *Journal of Agricultural and Resource Economics* 19(1): 141–60.

Chapter 6
Who Pays, Who Benefits?
An Analysis of Taxes and Expenditures in Oregon

Joseph Cortright [1]

Introduction

The Portland metropolitan area plays a key role in driving Oregon's economy. Job and population growth in the metropolitan area have reshaped the region, and the state's economy, in ways that are obvious to most Oregonians. Less obvious and less well understood is the metro area's role in funding the public services financed and provided by state government. In examining the fiscal contributions of the Portland metro area to the state budget, this report aims to shed light on the relationships between the state's largest metropolitan area and the rest of the state in the realm of expenditures for public services.

Part I of this chapter describes the methodology used in the analysis and the strengths and limitations of the data and methods. Many, but by no means all, state revenues and expenditures can be characterized as accruing from or benefiting a particular geographic area. This section explains the reliability of data and the important aspects of assumptions needed to undertake this analysis. Part II gives the reader a brief overview of public finance in Oregon, addressing how the state raises revenue and the major purposes to which public funds are allocated. This overview section also identifies which specific categories of expenditure are included in this report.

The heart of the analysis can be found in Parts III and IV. Part III analyzes the geographic origin of state revenues. It examines three major taxes and estimates the share of revenues from each that is provided by economic activity in the Portland metropolitan area. Part IV looks at two principal categories of state expenditure—K-12 education and health care—and estimates the share of state spending in each category that flows to the Portland metropolitan area. For each expenditure category, we present a summary fiscal-flow analysis that shows how much revenue is generated in the Portland area, how much is spent, and the net fiscal flow between the metropolitan area and the rest of the state.

Part V considers the implications of this analysis. Overall, there is a substantial net flow of resources from the metropolitan area to the remainder of Oregon. It seems apparent that the availability of public services in much of nonmetropolitan Oregon hinges vitally on the economic health of the Portland metropolitan area.

Part I. Research Approach

State government directly and indirectly provides a variety of public services for Oregon residents. Directly provided services include payment programs and services delivered by state agencies, such as road construction and medical care programs. Indirectly provided services include K-12 education, which is supported by state-shared revenues that are distributed to local areas by the state. These services are financed by a variety of taxes and fees imposed on state residents. A key premise underlying this study is that the tax revenues to pay for public services stem from economic activity. The state's ability to collect taxes is affected by the health of the economy in different parts of the state.

Geographical definitions

One of the defining characteristics of any regional economy is the flow of its most vital commodity—labor. The six counties that form the region are closely linked by commuting patterns. Data from the 2000 census show that 97 percent of all those who worked in the metropolitan area were also residents of the region, and a similar portion of the region's jobs were held by the region's residents.

Technical issues

A number of technical issues impede any effort to precisely measure the flow of public funds to various counties in the state. Perhaps the key impediment is that state budgeting and financial reporting systems are designed primarily for other purposes (planning overall expenditures, maintaining managerial control, assuring legal accountability for funds), and not for tracking funds by county. Another obstacle to constructing an internally consistent and integrated picture of revenues and expenditures is the variation in budget periods for different activities. Most taxes, for example, are paid on a calendar-year basis, while most expenditures are made on a fiscal-year basis. Some data on program activities are available quarterly or monthly, while others are only available yearly. In general, we have addressed this problem by constructing annual average revenue and expenditure information that corresponds to one-half of the 2007-2009 biennium. To simplify the comparison of data from different time periods, we have stated conclusions in percentage terms; e.g., the Portland metropolitan area is responsible for 54 percent of the revenue and 40 percent of the expenditures for a specific program.

Usually some percentage of the cost or benefit of a particular activity can be attributed to a specific geographic location. State aid for K-12 education can be identified for each school district in the state. However, expenditures for state central services for education, such as the operation of the Oregon Department of Education, which presumably support all schools throughout the state, are not apportioned by geography. In general, where the primary purpose of a specific program was to serve a population or provide services that could be identified on a geographic basis, we apportioned the central administrative costs of that function according to the geographic allocation we identified based on client population or program expenditures.

Limitations of this analysis

This study looks only at what economists would call the "first-order" effects of the differential in the geographic origin of benefits and costs of various state services. One effect of net fiscal flows from one part of the state to another over a period of time will be the indirect economic activity induced by shifting more government spending to one part of the state than would otherwise occur. For example, an increase in state spending in a given county may result in more jobs and income in the local economy, more income re-spent locally (the multiplier effect), and ultimately higher state personal income-tax collections. We do not estimate these second-order effects as part of this study.

Similarly, this analysis focuses on the direct and immediate payers of taxes and recipients of benefits; we do not attempt to further trace either the burden of taxation or the benefit of expenditure from the initial source of payment. In many cases, the benefits of certain expenditures accrue to citizens living in a wider area than the area in which the money is actually spent. For example, K-12 education expenditures may occur in one county in one year, but the benefits of that education to the student and the state may accrue over years. And some of the benefits, like a better-educated population, accrue to citizens who ultimately live elsewhere in the state or even outside the state.

Likewise, the actual burden of taxes may be borne by someone other than the initial payer. Businesses, for example, may shift the costs of taxation to customers living elsewhere. Finally, while we believe that tax revenues are largely generated from the economic activity that occurs in different counties, we recognize that there are many important economic interdependencies between Portland-area counties and other parts of the state. These economic interrelationships are well explored in chapters 2, 5, and 9 in this volume. Taxes paid by businesses in the Portland area are driven in part by the demand for services created by rural economic activity, as when people travel to Portland for health care or shopping, or when wheat is transshipped through the Port of Portland. Similarly, taxes paid in rural Oregon are driven in part by the tourism and recreation activities of Portland businesses and by the demand for rural resources, like lumber and electricity, from urban markets.

Part II. Fiscal Overview

This section of the report provides an overview of the major state taxes and spending programs, excluding certain categories of spending and revenues that do not meet the criteria we established for inclusion in our analysis. Our analysis of state government's impact on the Oregon economy focuses on the state general fund, which is the chief source of financing for most state-financed public services, along with several other specialized funds financed by dedicated revenues, including the gasoline and road-use taxes, payroll taxes, tobacco taxes, and lottery proceeds.

Oregon's general-fund budget consists of about $15.1 billion in the 2007-2009 biennium. Table 1 shows the distribution of general-fund expenditures by major program area. General funds can be employed with wide discretion by the governor and legislature to fund any major purpose of state government, and go mostly to finance education, human-resource programs, and public safety, which together account for more than 90 percent of all general-fund expenditures.

K-12 Education	6,245.0
Oregon Health Plan	1,565.4
All Other	7,296.6
GF/LF Total	15,107.0

Table 1. Total general-fund and lottery-fund spending, 2007-2009 biennium (millions of dollars). Source: Oregon Legislative Fiscal Office.

Many state programs are financed by revenues from taxes dedicated by the state constitution or by statute to particular purposes. For example, gasoline taxes and other road-use taxes may constitutionally be used only to build and maintain roads, bridges, and highways. In the aggregate the state expends about $15 billion per biennium (about $7.5 billion annually) to provide public services from the general fund and the major sources of other fund revenues described here. Together, K-12 education and the Oregon Health Plan make up about 52 percent of these expenditures.

The taxes and fees that fund these expenditures are listed in tables 2 and 3. Table 2 shows the major sources of revenue for the general fund for the 2007-2009 biennium; total biennial amounts are shown in the first column of the table and the average annual level of tax revenue for the biennium is shown in the second column. Actual annual levels of revenue vary; an average was calculated for ease of comparison with expenditures.

	Biennial	Annual
Personal Income Tax	11,143.1	5,571.6
Corporate Income Tax	857.3	428.7
Lottery Funds	1,152.0	576.0
All Other	1,954.6	977.3
Total	15,107.0	7,553.5

Table 2. Total general-fund and lottery-fund revenues, 2007-2009 biennium (millions of dollars). Source: Oregon Legislative Fiscal Office.

Source	Total	Metro amount	Metro share
Personal Income Tax	5,571.6	3,073.6	55.2%
Corporate Excise Tax	428.7	243.2	56.7%
Melded	6,000.3	3,316.8	55.3%

Table 3. Estimated source of general-fund revenue, by tax, 2007-2009 biennium, annualized (millions of dollars). Note: Revenues apportioned according to most recent data on sources of revenues; i.e., 2007-2009 income-tax revenue apportioned according to 2006 data on source of income-tax payments. Source: Department of Revenue data, Impresa calculations.

Part III. Revenues

In this section we examine the geographic distribution of general-fund and lottery-fund revenues collected by state government. This analysis of the sources of revenue provides the basis for estimating, program by program, the fiscal flows to and from the metropolitan area that are presented in Part IV. We gather data on the geographic pattern of payments for each distinct source of revenue. Because the publication of these data necessarily lags behind the collection of revenue, we use data from prior years rather than from the current biennium, but we use the most recent available data to estimate the share of each revenue source originating from economic activity in the Portland metropolitan area. We then multiply this share, expressed as a percentage, of the annual revenue flow for the 1997-99 biennium to compute the dollar amount raised in the Portland metropolitan area.

Along with revenues from state personal and corporate income taxes, the general fund receives revenue from excise taxes on tobacco; from the sale and taxation of liquor, beer, and wine; and from other sources. A detailed description of each of the major revenue sources is provided in the following sections. Overall, we estimate that more than 55 percent of general-fund revenues arise from taxes and fees generated from economic activity in the Portland metropolitan area.

Personal income taxes

The personal income tax is Oregon's largest source of revenue, raising more than $5 billion in tax year 2008. It is paid by Oregon households based on their total income, adjusted for deductions and tax credits. Tax rates range from 5 percent to 9 percent of taxable income; the effective tax rate averages about 5.6 percent on all personal income. The Oregon Department of Revenue tabulates state tax returns by county and reports the number of returns filed, exemptions claimed, income reported, and tax paid, as well as other information, for each county.

Out-of-state residents who work in Oregon are required to pay Oregon income tax. The biggest impact of this provision is on residents of Clark County, Washington, who work in the Portland metropolitan area. In calendar year 2008, the most recent year for which data are available, Clark County residents paid about $134 million in Oregon personal income taxes on income they earned in Oregon. According to the 2000 census, 41,000 Clark County residents commuted to jobs in Oregon; nearly 99 percent of them held jobs in

Region	1985	1996	2006
State	1,078	2,602	5,571
Metro	573	1,443	3,073
Metro Share	53.2%	55.5%	55.2%

Table 4. Personal income-tax receipts statewide and in the metro area, 1985, 1996, and 2006 (millions of dollars). Note: Here the metro area includes Clark County, Washington. Source: Oregon Department of Revenue data, Impresa calculations.

one of the five counties in the Oregon portion of the metropolitan statistical area. Table 4 shows income-tax receipts for selected years. For the past two decades, the Portland metropolitan area has accounted for a majority of state personal income-tax collections.

Personal income-tax collections for the Portland metropolitan area are significantly higher than the region's share of the state's population (45 percent), for a variety of reasons. Incomes per person are higher in the Portland metro area than elsewhere in the state: the metro area accounted for 58 percent of all Oregon wage and salary income earned in 2008. In addition, wages per worker are substantially higher than elsewhere in the state—about $44,000 per year in the metro area versus $34,000 in the rest of the state.

Two features of the tax system further increase the share of taxes paid by metro-area residents. First, Oregon has a progressive income tax, meaning higher-income households are taxed more per dollar of income than are lower-income households. Second, more of the income earned in the metro area is subject to taxation, while areas outside Portland are much more reliant on sources of income that are not generally subject to personal income taxes. For example, 20 percent of nonmetro income comes from largely untaxed government transfer payments such as Social Security, Medicaid, and welfare, while only 13 percent of metro area income comes from these sources. In addition, the income earned by Clark County residents from jobs they hold in Oregon—which are overwhelmingly in the metro area—is added to Portland-area tax payments.

Corporate excise taxes

The corporate excise tax is assessed against the net income of corporations doing business in Oregon. It is the second-largest source of revenue to the general fund, providing approximately $420 million annually as of the 2007-2009 biennium. Corporations pay a flat 6.6 percent tax rate on their net Oregon income; for corporations that operate in several states, net income is apportioned to Oregon for tax purposes according to a formula based on the proportion of the firm's sales in Oregon. Only corporations with net income are required to pay the corporate tax—those that lose money or break even generally have no tax liability.

Unlike households, whose members typically reside in a single county, many Oregon businesses, especially the state's largest (which are also the largest corporate taxpayers) operate in a number of counties. Large businesses with a statewide presence, like banks, utilities, retail chains, and some manufacturing firms, file a single corporate income-tax return covering all of their operations throughout the state. While these returns may list the principal location or headquarters of the firm as a filing address, this does not represent the only or even the primary location of business.

We wanted to develop an approach that avoided the obvious pitfall of assigning a firm's entire personal income tax to the one county in which its headquarters was located, and apportioned corporate income according to the distribution of a company's various economic activities around the state. The ideal means of allocating revenue by county within the state would be to examine individual corporate tax returns and to allocate revenue by county using some method similar to the state's three-factor formula for allocating income among states. However, individual company records are confidential, and the work required to apportion the net income of hundreds of firms is beyond the scope of this project.

As an alternative, we allocated corporate net income according to the distribution of industry employment in different parts of the state. Data from the Oregon Department of Revenue for tax year 2005 show the total amount of corporate taxes paid, by industry, using the firm's reported three-digit North American Industry Classification System (NAICS) code. Using information on the distribution of private-sector employment by the same classification published by the Oregon Employment Department, we estimated the share of each industry's employment that was located in each county in Oregon.

Table 5 shows the results of this analysis. Based on an allocation weighted according to the Portland-area employment in each three-digit NAICS code, Portland-area businesses accounted for $163 million of the $287 million in total corporate income tax paid in 2005, or nearly 57 percent of the statewide total. The Portland area accounts for about 54 percent of the state's employ-

State	286,946
Metro	162,823
Metro Share	56.7%

Table 5. Estimated corporate income-tax collections statewide and in the metro area, 2006 (millions of dollars). Source: Oregon Department of Revenue and Employment Department data, Impresa calculations.

Game	Statewide	Metro	Metro Share
Traditional Games	$187,833,462	$90,347,895	48.1%
Video Lottery	$484,388,062	$269,804,151	55.7%
All Lottery Games	$672,221,524	$360,152,046	53.6%

Table 6. Net earnings from lottery games statewide and in the metro area, 2007. Source: Oregon Lottery.

ment and about 58 percent of its total wages. Because economic activity is more concentrated in the metro area than elsewhere, the Portland metro area pays a disproportionately large share of the corporate tax compared to other parts of the state.

Lottery revenues

In 1984, Oregon voters authorized the establishment of a state-run lottery, with net proceeds initially dedicated to funding the state's economic-development efforts. Lottery games now generate more than $350 million per year in net state revenues. Broadly speaking, the lottery's games can be divided into two major categories: traditional games and video lottery. Traditional lottery games include instant scratch tickets, lotto games with once- or twice-weekly drawings and large cumulative jackpots (for example, Megabucks and Powerball), and keno, which offers drawings every five minutes. Video lottery games consist of video poker terminals, which the Oregon Lottery has operated since 1992 in bars and taverns around the state, as well as newer games. Video poker is the Oregon Lottery's largest revenue producer, generating more than 77 percent of net revenue.

The Portland area contributes disproportionately to state revenues from both traditional lottery games and video lottery games (table 6). The higher incomes in the metropolitan area translate directly into higher lottery sales, and urban areas in general tend to have higher rates of play of lottery games than do rural areas. In addition, Portland may have the advantage of a lack of competition (there is no video lottery in Washington), whereas lottery games in many rural areas compete with Native American casinos.

Part IV. Fiscal Flows in K-12 Education and Health Services

Education

The single largest item in the state budget is financial support for K-12 education, provided from the state school fund, supported by a combination of

Source	Amount	Share
General Fund	5,590,757,521	89.48%
Lottery	654,142,231	10.47%
Other	3,247,438	0.05%
Total	6,248,147,190	100.00%

Table 7. State school fund appropriations in dollars, 2007-2009.
Source: Oregon Legislative Fiscal Office.

general funds and lottery funds. Measure 5, enacted in 1990, radically changed the way Oregon finances K-12 education. The measure mandated a reduction in property tax support for schools and required the state to make up revenue shortfalls. Before Measure 5, the state provided about 30 percent of local school funding. By 1997-98, it provided about 70 percent. For the 2007-2009 biennium, the legislature appropriated $6.2 billion for K-12 education. As shown in table 7, nearly 90 percent of the revenue came from the general fund, and nearly all of the remainder from state lottery revenues.

Monies in the state school fund are distributed to school districts based on a complex formula that considers the number of students in each district, the socioeconomic status of students, the experience level of teachers, and transportation costs. Over the past several years, the state has adjusted its formula to move toward the equalization of per-pupil expenditures in different districts across the state. As a result, increases in state aid have disproportionately been directed to historically lower-spending districts in order to bring them closer to the statewide average spending level.

Oregon's current system of school finance transfers significant revenues out of the Portland metropolitan area to support the costs of providing schooling in the rest of the state. Is this large outflow a recent development? We examined the historical allocation of state school support for two earlier years. The 1978-79 school year corresponds roughly to the late-1970s peak in the Oregon economy. The 1989-90 school year corresponds to the period

	1978-1979	1989-1990	1998-1999	2006-2007
Statewide Spending	341	566	1,970	3,123
Metro Share	146 (42.8%)	225 (39.8%)	812 (41.2%)	1,721 (42.9%)
Statewide Revenue	341	566	1,970	3,123
Metro Share	177 (52.0%)	307 (54.3%)	1,087 (52.2%)	1,340 (55.1%)
Outflow	(31)	(82)	(275)	(381)

Table 8. State school support, selected fiscal years (millions of current dollars). Source: Oregon Department of Education and Oregon Department of Revenue data, Impresa calculations.

immediately before the adoption of Measure 5 tax limits, which led, over a five-year period, to the restructuring of Oregon school finance. Table 8 shows the distribution of state aid for K-12 schools to the metropolitan area and the rest of the state for these two earlier years, along with comparable data for the current school year. The annual net outflow of revenue from the Portland metropolitan area to support statewide school finance was about $31 million in the late 1970s, about $82 million just prior to Measure 5, and about $275 million in 1999.

Health services

The largest program area of the Department of Human Resources is the provision of health services, including the Oregon Health Plan, which is the largest component of the state's health-services expenditures. The Oregon Health Plan provides financial assistance to low-income families to pay for health and medical care, as well as mental-health and public-health services. Funding for the Oregon Health Plan and related programs comes from a combination of federal funds, general funds, and tobacco taxes.

For the 2007-2009 biennium, the estimated total general-fund spending on the Oregon Health Plan and related medical care programs was $1,521 million (table 9). We based our estimate on the pattern of spending for the Oregon Health Plan; the Department of Human Resources tracks enrollment by county and tabulates expenditures by the enrollee's county of residence. All told, about 42.8 percent of expenditures were made in the Portland metropolitan area.

State	1,337
Metro	571
Metro Share	42.8%

Table 9. Oregon Health Plan expenditures statewide and in the metro area, 2006 (millions of dollars). Source: Oregon Department of Human Resources.

Part V. Implications

It is apparent that the Portland metropolitan area is a major contributor to state government's fiscal well-being. In every major program area examined, taxpayers in the metro area pay far more in state taxes and fees than residents of the area receive in state services and shared revenues. The reasons for this net outflow are firmly rooted in Oregon's fundamental economic and fiscal realities. The most important factor is the robust economy of the Portland metropolitan area. Per capita incomes in the Portland area are 30 percent higher than in the rest of the state. Jobs are more plentiful, wages and salaries are higher, and unemployment is lower.

The economic strength of the Portland area alone would probably produce a net fiscal flow from the metro area to the balance of the state. The effect is amplified by the state's heavy reliance on a relatively progressive personal income tax to finance most state services. The bulk of state income taxes are paid by high-income households; in Oregon, these households are found disproportionately in the metropolitan area. The economic strength of the metropolitan area is equally important in driving state expenditures. Higher rates of unemployment and poverty outside the Portland area create the need for additional income support payments and social services. Poverty rates are 30 percent higher outside the metro area, and government transfer payments provide half again as large a share of personal income.

No individual taxpayer or group of taxpayers necessarily receives back in services the same share or amount paid in taxes, but as a group, high-income households pay far more in taxes than they receive in benefits from state-supported programs. Income redistribution is not only an explicit aim of Oregon's income tax structure but an implicit feature of many state government policies. The net flow of public resources from areas with many high-income households to areas with many lower-income households is the logical outcome of the policy decisions the state has made in setting up its tax and spending systems.

It appears that the magnitude of fiscal flows from the Portland area to the rest of the state has increased in the past decade for two reasons. First, the gap between urban and rural Oregon, measured by per capita income, has widened appreciably during that time. Second, because of the effects of Measure 5, the state has taken on a much larger share of the cost of financing public services, notably K-12 education.

The existence of these major fiscal flows from the Portland metropolitan area points up the critical dependence that all Oregonians, including those living in rural communities, have on the continued success of the Portland metropolitan economy. Absent the high incomes and associated taxes generated by the Portland area, Oregon's fiscal situation would be far worse than it is.

A parallel implication of this analysis is that the state has a strong interest in promoting income growth in rural Oregon. Fiscal disparities between the

Portland area and the rest of the state are fundamentally a product of lower incomes in smaller urban and rural communities. While residents of these areas may never catch up to the level of income in the Portland area, raising incomes in nonmetro Oregon would help minimize fiscal flows, both by raising the share of taxes generated and lowering demand for many public services.

Bibliography

Cortright, Joseph. 1999. Oregon Fiscal Flow Analysis. Portland: Impresa, Inc.

Culver, Xann (Oregon Department of Revenue). 2008. C-Corp tax returns by three-digit NAICS code, tax year 2005 (personal communication).

Lawhorn, Melissa (Oregon Department of Human Resources). 2007 Oregon Health Plan data by county (personal communication).

Legislative Fiscal Office. 2007 Budget Highlights. http://www.leg.state.or.us/comm/lfo/2007-09_budget/2007-09%20Budget%20Highlights.pdf. Consulted September 7, 2008.

Meissner, Marlene (Oregon Lottery). 2008. County-by-county sales data for video lottery and traditional lottery games, July 2007 through June 2008 (personal communication).

Oregon Department of Education. 2008. Actual Revenues by Fund and Source. http://www.ode.state.or.us/data/reports/toc.aspx#finance/funding.

Oregon Department of Revenue. 2008. Oregon Personal Income Tax Annual Statistics, 2006, Publication 101-406-08. http://www.oregon.gov/DOR/STATS/101-406-08-toc.shtml.

Oregon Employment Department. 2007. Covered employment and payrolls, 2006. Unpublished data.

Oregon Lottery Commission. 2007. Year-to-date Sales Report. http://info.oregonlottery.org/033.htm.

Chapter 7
The Politics of One Oregon
Causes and Consequences of the Rural-Urban Divide and Prospects for Overcoming It

Richard A. Clucas
Mark Henkels
Brent S. Steel

Oregon's state and local governments face many challenges today that complicate their tasks of sustaining current programs in both rural and urban areas and of finding politically acceptable solutions to the state's most pressing policy concerns. How public officials respond to these challenges will affect the long-term viability of state and local governments.

Economic change has long been among the most perplexing of these challenges. Over the past century Oregon has evolved from a rural economy based on agriculture and natural resources to an economy that is largely urbanized and industrial. In recent decades the state has developed into a postindustrial society, one in which the economy is heavily dependent on knowledge-based industries and most citizens are employed in service sector jobs. The state has also witnessed dramatic demographic shifts, continued urbanization, increased globalization, and important technological advances. These and other changes have required state and local governments to rethink their policies in the face of new problems and political demands. As Roger Kemp, a leading expert on state and local politics, puts it: "Evolving societal conditions and public perceptions have created trends that require communities to change in order to meet the public's expectation for effective and equitable governance" (Kemp 2001, 1).

Perhaps the most difficult challenge for governance in Oregon is that these broader forces have affected Oregon's rural and urban communities differently, creating a dramatic political divide between different regions of the state. As the urban areas have generally moved into a postindustrial society, many rural areas retaining strong agrarian roots have seen their economic base deteriorate. As a result, rural and urban areas of the state hold considerably different perspectives on society and the role that government ought to play. Demographic shifts, technological advances, and other changes have reinforced these economic disparities, making the political divide between rural and urban areas even more pronounced.

If state and local governments are to adapt to the challenges they confront, it is important that political leaders understand how these broader forces have reshaped Oregon's politics. In this chapter we identify the driving forces of the rural-urban conflict and discuss how these forces have shaped modern Oregon politics. In exploring some of the causes of polarization, we hope to identify areas of common concern and to suggest possible strategies for cooperation.

The Forces behind the Divide

Post-industrial society

Over the past four decades, many social scientists have tried to understand why Western democracies have seen so many political changes since the 1960s, including the rise of new social movements, increased disillusionment with established political parties, and the emergence of a variety of new issues into political debate, from the environment to feminism to human rights. One of the primary explanations is that these political changes have grown out of economic change. In particular, many scholars who conduct research comparing nations argue that the recent political changes in Western democracies reflect the transformation of Western economies into what is referred to as a "postindustrial society." While scholars disagree on the characteristics of a postindustrial society, a few commonly agreed-on features can be identified (Bell 1973; Bellah 1985; Inglehart 1997):

- Economic dominance of the service sector over manufacturing and agriculture;
- A high degree of economic activity based on an educated workforce employing scientific knowledge and technology;
- Increasing population growth and employment in urban areas and subsequent decline in many rural areas;

- Unprecedented societal affluence; and
- A high level of political participation in society, including the rise of new social causes and movements.

Although there are debates within this literature, many studies have found that the postindustrial theory provides a good explanation for political change across the globe. While there are some cross-cultural differences in how these changes affect individual countries (for example, Americans are more individualistic and suspicious of government than Scandinavians are), the development of the postindustrial society is considered to broadly impact politics, making the postindustrial nations different from industrial and agricultural-based nations. At the heart of this theory is the argument that "economic development, cultural change, and political change go together in coherent, and to some extent, even predictable patterns" (Inglehart 1997, 5). Table 1 identifies some of the key socioeconomic differences that scholars have discovered when comparing advanced industrial countries with more agrarian and industrial ones.

While the literature on postindustrial society grew out of research by scholars who compared and contrasted development among nations, the theoretical argument provides a good explanation for the political trends that have been occurring in Oregon. All the commonly agreed-upon features found

	Agricultural-based society	Industrial society	Post-industrial society
ECONOMIC FEATURES			
Sectoral dominance	Agriculture and natural resource extraction	Manufacturing	Services
Systemic character	Labor intensive	Capital intensive	Knowledge intensive
Technical change	Slow	Rapid	Exponential
Material condition	Poverty/subsistence	Rising productivity	Relative affluence
SOCIAL FEATURES			
Population	Rural	Urban	Megalopolitan
Population growth	High	Moderating	Low or negative
Community	Intimate	Eroding	Impersonal
Dominant values	Basic/survival needs	Material security	Post-materialist values

Table 1. Socioeconomic characteristics of different types of societies.

in postindustrial societies, and which we identified above, can also be found in Oregon, especially in the more urban parts of the state, which tend to be the most populated and most affluent, with the highest level of employment and the greatest concentration of high-tech businesses (Clucas et al. 2005, 9). Urban residents also exhibit the most support for many recent social movements, including the anti-globalization and environmental movements.

The rural areas of the state do exhibit some characteristics of postindustrial society; for example, the largest job occupation in eastern Oregon is in the service sector (Yohannan 2005). Yet the rural areas have not enjoyed the same level of economic prosperity and job growth as have the metropolitan areas, and many have faced continued economic challenges since the early 1980s. In 2005, the Portland metropolitan area had the state's lowest unemployment rate, 5.7 percent, whereas southern and eastern Oregon, the most rural parts of the state, had the highest, 6.7 and 8.0 percent, respectively (Oregon Office of Economic Analysis 2007, 44). Even during the worst economic conditions since the Great Depression, these patterns persist in 2010, with many rural counties suffering jobless rates exceeding 15 percent (seasonally adjusted), and many Willamette Valley counties having significantly lower rates (Read 2010). Clearly, the transition of the state into a postindustrial society has not been beneficial to the rural regions.

The rise of the postindustrial society is considered significant because it can lead to important cultural changes, which in turn influence politics. Many social scientists argue that, like the previous shift from an agricultural to an industrial society, the shift from an industrial to a postindustrial society in many nations has produced a fundamental cultural realignment. It has profoundly reshaped people's value structures, causing many to become more concerned with what psychologist Abraham Maslow has termed higher-order needs, such as social affiliation and quality-of-life issues. These higher-order needs have supplanted more fundamental subsistence needs, such as concern for health and safety, in motivating individual and societal behavior (Maslow 1959). People in postindustrial societies typically show greater concern for quality-of-life issues and environmental protection, more tolerance for nontraditional lifestyles, and stronger support for freedom on moral issues such as abortion, gay rights, and women's rights (Inglehart 1977 and 1997, Inglehart and Weizel 2010; Steger et al. 1989). This is especially true of younger people. Members of "Generation X" (born between 1961 and 1982) and especially of the "Millennium Generation" (born after 1982) are significantly more engaged in their communities through internships, volunteer work, and community action groups than are older people (Dalton 2009; Winograd and Hais 2009). In addition, they are significantly more tolerant and accepting of gay rights and racial and ethnic diversity and are more concerned about the environment. With generational replacement, the rising prevalence of such new attitudes places new demands on state and local government (Simon et al. 2011).

This general pattern of development from industrial to postindustrial society is consistent with Oregon's experience. In Oregon's early history, the principal issues of concern were basic nutrition, shelter, access to water, safe routes of travel, safety of person and property, and the like. As Oregon became more industrialized, new concerns arose, including unsafe workplaces, poor health services, dangerous waste disposal, and inadequate public education systems. In more recent decades, residents have become more attentive to higher-order concerns revolving around quality of life, the environment, and nontraditional lifestyles.

The emergence of the postindustrial society has affected rural and urban areas quite differently, and this, we believe, is at the root of our political divide. In the urban areas, where the postindustrial economy is the most advanced, we find the greatest support for these new ideas, whereas rural voters have decidedly different opinions. Random household surveys in 2008 and 2010 shed some light on these value changes (table 2). Drawing from research by

Values	Portland Metro	All Urban Respondents	Rural Respondents
Materialist			
2008	17%	18%	26%
2010	18%	20%	28%
Mixed			
2008	49%	53%	57%
2010	44%	53%	53%
Postmaterialist			
2008	34%	29%	17%
2010	38%	27%	19%
2008	n = 346	n = 537	n = 137
2010	n = 607	n = 952	n = 233

Table 2. Rural and urban citizens and postmaterialist values (percent). Note: The random-sample household survey of Oregon citizens was conducted by researchers at Oregon State University during September and October 2008. Responses were received from 674 households out of 1,200 contacts possible for a response rate of 56 percent. Portland, n = 346; All urban, n = 537; Rural, n = 137. The second survey was conducted in fall 2010.

	Materialist	Mixed	Postmaterialist
Very liberal	6	4	21
Liberal	6	22	34
Moderate	50	41	23
Conservative	32	28	20
Very conservative	7	5	2
	n = 161	n = 497	n = 224

Table 3. Post-materialist values and self-identified political ideology (percent). Note: The random-sample household survey of Oregon citizens was conducted by researchers at Oregon State University during September and October 2008. Responses were received from 674 households out of 1,200 contacts possible for a response rate of 56 percent.

Ronald Inglehart on postindustrial societies, the survey identified three types of values (materialist, postmaterialist, and mixed—that is, individuals holding a combination of postmaterialist and materialist values)[1], and revealed that postmaterialist values are more prevalent in metropolitan areas, while materialist values are more prevalent in rural areas even in a time of severe economic conditions and near-Depression levels of unemployment (Crandall and Weber 2005). Post-materialists are much more willing to identify them-

Percent strongly supporting	Materialists	Mixed	Post-materialists
A. Pay equity—equal pay for equal work	69	76	88
B. Comparable worth—equal pay for comparable work	37	53	66
C. Affirmative action—for employment in business or government	8	18	34
D. Affirmative action—for access to higher education	11	23	41
E. Title IX (9)—prohibits sex discrimination in education (academics and athletics)	33	48	69
F. Parental leave—government legislation providing for parental leave from work	20	36	65
G. Day care—government-subsidized day care for working parents	13	26	42
H. Women in combat—allowing women in the military to participate in combat	19	25	42

Table 4. Postmaterialist values and support for gender-equity policies. Note: Results are based on a random-sample survey of Oregon households conducted Spring 2004 by researchers at Oregon State University. Responses were received from 1,354 households for a response rate of 52 percent.

selves as liberal or very liberal and to express strong support for gender-equity policies than are those with materialist and mixed-value orientations (tables 3 and 4). It is clear that a person with a postmaterialist values orientation would likely have distinctly different political preferences from someone with a materialist or mixed orientation.

With a more affluent workforce and a more robust economy, the urban areas have come to adopt many of the values of the postindustrial society. Rural citizens, many of whom have faced severe economic problems over the past few decades, are not as supportive of those values. The differential pace of development of the postindustrial society in Oregon is the most significant factor in the existence of the rural-urban political divide. However, other related factors have also been important: urbanization, demographic change, globalization, technological advances, and a changing environmental ethic. We discuss these factors next.

Urbanization

When it joined the Union in 1849, Oregon was a rural state with a population of 52,465. It has been transformed to a significantly urban state with a population of nearly 3.8 million. After growing relatively slowly throughout in the nineteenth century, the pace of urbanization picked up dramatically in the twentieth. Today more than 65 percent of Oregon's population lives in urban areas (U.S. Census). Increased urbanization is a key characteristic of a postindustrial society, and it is important to consider its impact on Oregon politics.

The migration of people from rural to urban and suburban areas is typically driven by the departure of the most highly educated workers and skilled younger residents from rural areas to seek jobs or further education (Deavers, personal communication). This migration has caused rural populations to decline and urban populations to swell. Continuing growth of Oregon's urban and suburban areas has boosted employment in the service sector, which today accounts for about 82 percent of all Oregon jobs today. Post-industrial cities are characterized by very high levels of service-sector employment, such as in the health, education, financial, and technology industries. Concomitantly, employment in the natural-resource-extraction sector, which historically has been important in rural communities, has declined to less than 1 percent of the contemporary (non farm) labor force, leading to rural migration to urban areas for economic reasons (Oregon Economic and Community Development

Department). Without the same diverse economic base as urban areas enjoy, rural communities have found themselves facing higher unemployment and poverty rates.

Increased urbanization has had an important impact on Oregon politics by shifting political power toward urban and suburban centers and away from rural areas (Beale and Fuguitt 1990), to the extent that many rural residents feel their voices on policy matters are drowned out by the interests of urban areas (Bates and Bates 1996). Urbanization has led to the rise of different policy priorities for rural and urban residents. While rural areas must grapple with economic problems and a shrinking population, urban areas confront their own challenges, including escalating land prices, a decline in affordable housing, growing traffic congestion, more-expensive construction costs, and greater demands for a variety of inner-city services, from expanded social services to improved public safety to better transportation systems (Simon et al. 2011). In short, growing urbanization means residents of rural and urban areas confront considerably different problems and therefore have different expectations about public policy.

Demographic change

Other important demographic changes over the past two decades have helped reinforce the divide created by the postindustrial society. Among the most significant is the growth in the state's Latino population. Historically, the metropolitan areas have been the most ethnically diverse parts of the state. The growing migration of Latinos into the state has made these areas even more diverse. From 2000 to 2007, Multnomah and Washington were among the top ninety counties nationwide in Latino population growth, witnessing a 50 percent increase in the number of Latino residents. Combined, those two counties accounted for almost 40 percent of the state's Latino population in 2007 (Pew Hispanic Center 2008). In addition, more than half of the state's sixty-six thousand African-Americans live in Portland (Mapstats). The growing diversity of the urban areas makes for greater demands on social services and more-diverse opinions on public policy matters than is found in rural areas.

In general, the increased demand on social services in more diverse communities stems from important socioeconomic and demographic differences among racial and ethnic groups, including average age, birthrate, education level, and income. For example, in a community composed primarily of older white residents, there may be pressure on policymakers to address such issues as health care and property taxes. In a more diverse community, residents may be concerned not only with these issues but with public education and the availability of community programs for those in mid-life.

However, the rise in Latino population is also a rural phenomenon, occurring in almost every county in Oregon. For example, Hood River, Malheur, and Morrow counties now are more than 25 percent Latino, the highest percentage in the state. The growth in Latino populations brings issues into these rural communities that until now have been more common to urban areas. As a result, the demographic shift may eventually close some of the gap between rural and urban areas in attitudes toward government, as the social-service issues surrounding Latino populations become more similar in urban and rural settings.

Another important demographic trend has been the aging of Oregon's rural population. In general, the median age of state residents has grown sharply over the past few decades, from just over thirty in 1980 to thirty-nine in 2007, and many rural counties have populations older than the statewide average. In 2007, the median age in Multnomah County was 37.2 years, while twelve eastern and coastal rural counties had populations with a median age of forty-four years or higher (Northwest Area Foundation). Rural governments confront a population with generally greater needs for social services for senior citizens, and less tolerance for tax increases. Moreover, because postindustrial values tend to be strongest among young people, the age differences among the counties reinforces the regional divide.

Globalization and economic change

"Globalization" means the current worldwide expansion of economic markets in a very broad range of goods and services. A global economy is a harsh competitive environment for local communities as they try to attract and retain businesses and jobs. Many rural communities are unable to afford the tax concessions and economic-development subsidies that wealthier communities can offer to potential employers. The influx of chain stores such as Wal-Mart threatens locally owned businesses, often weakening community culture and reducing investment in local enterprises. While these problems can occur in urban settings, they are especially pronounced in rural communities because there is less economic diversity there to start with.

Technological advances

The continuous growth in information technology is one of the key characteristics of postindustrial societies. Urban communities typically have a more highly developed technological infrastructure than rural communities, and are therefore best positioned to attract the sorts of knowledge-based businesses that characterize postindustrial societies. Infrastructure is also becoming an important concern of state and local governments, as citizens increasingly expect to use the Internet to communicate with public officials, access government information, and submit a variety of important documents. State and local governments in Oregon have tried to meet this growing demand by expanding their presence on the Web. Today, many Oregon residents can pay their property taxes, apply for various permits, make court payments, get transportation updates, and learn about local government activities online. State and local governments also use the Internet to engage citizens in the policy-making process by providing residents with the opportunity to learn and comment on important policy questions.

Citizens living in urban areas are more likely to use the Internet than are rural citizens (Rainie et al. 2004, 2005). In addition, Scott (2005) found in a study of municipal web sites that "city size and scale matter in achieving overall Web site quality" (161). Smaller and more rural local governments have far fewer resources and more limited expertise to develop and maintain Web sites and Internet services, resulting in an access gap. Thus, the promise that these new technologies offer in delivering enhanced governmental services and greater public involvement in policy making remains in question for many rural communities. The difficulties confronting rural government can be seen in a 2005-2006 survey of Oregon city executives, which found that cities with fewer than twenty-five hundred residents have more limited online capacity than larger cities.[2] Although no studies have yet addressed how this disparity is affecting Oregon's political divide, evidence from national research suggests the presence of a digital divide can reinforce existing political and economic inequalities (Mossberger et al. 2003; Simon et al. 2011).

A changing environmental ethic

The final trend that has helped to create the regional divide has been the emergence of a new paradigm for thinking about the natural environment, one that has found much stronger support among urban than rural residents.

Its development is closely tied to the rise of postmaterialist values, and its impact has been so important in shaping Oregon politics that it is worth considering separately.

The start of the twentieth century witnessed rapid growth in the number of citizens interested in the conservation of natural resources. This concern was based on anthropocentric premises—that is, on a human-oriented view of nature in which human needs and wants are given priority in natural-resource management. Supporters of conservation call for the intelligent use of natural resources so that they can continue to benefit future generations of people. The primary aim of conservation policy is to allow nature to be used to meet human needs, whether for the development of commodities, such as lumber or food, or for aesthetic or spiritual benefits, such as wilderness preservation and outdoor recreation.

By the early 1970s, however, a new environmental paradigm had emerged across the nation and in many of Oregon's communities, one that is more centered on biological or ecological processes (Dunlap and Mertig 1992; Milbrath 1996). The biocentric approach elevates the value of all natural organisms, species, and ecosystems to center stage and, in some versions, makes the health of the planet's entire environmental system the focus of moral consideration. Advocates of this orientation do not ignore human needs, but they place them in a larger ecological context. Adherents of this view

Percent agreeing and strongly agreeing	Portland Metro	All Urban	Rural
A. The so-called "ecological crisis" facing humankind has been greatly exaggerated.	27	31	33
B. Humans have the right to modify the natural environment to suit their needs.	27	32	38
C. Humans were meant to rule over the rest of nature.	26	31	40
D. The balance of nature is very delicate and easily upset by human activities.	78	71	54
E. We are approaching the limit of people the earth can support.	52	49	41
F. Plants and animals have as much right as humans to exist.	70	68	53

Table 5. Rural and urban support for a new ecological paradigm. Note: The random-sample household survey of Oregon citizens was conducted by researchers at Oregon State University during September and October 2008.

tend to assume that there is intrinsic value in protecting pristine ecosystems, wilderness areas, wildlife, and indigenous plants.

While there is support for this new environmental ethic throughout Oregon, it has been particularly strong in urban areas (Table 2). Many urban residents have opinions on natural-resource issues and land-use policy that are quite different from those of many rural residents, who remain more supportive of conservation policies. With the increased urbanization of the state and the growing concentration of power in urban areas, the state has become willing to adopt environmental-protection rules that are unpopular in rural communities, which has helped to exacerbate the regional divide (Dietrich 1992; Carroll 1995).

Impact on Oregon Politics

The late 1960s into the mid-1970s are often depicted by political observers as a golden era in Oregon politics, a time in which political leaders were able to work together to pass some of the state's most innovative policy reforms, such as the beach bill and comprehensive statewide land-use policies. Writing in the mid-1970s, historian Gordon Dodds said: "Oregon was becoming known for the substance rather than the structure of its politics" (Dodds 1977; see also Bodine 1993). Yet since at least the mid-1990s, the state's politics has been characterized not by cooperation and consensus but by conflict.

The rise of the postindustrial society and the emergence of these other forces have been significant because they have helped produce this conflict. What is particularly important is that these forces have pushed the state through a partisan realignment, one in which rural voters have grown increasingly supportive of the Republican Party and urban voters more supportive of the Democratic Party. To be sure, there are many urban Republicans and rural Democrats in Oregon today. Furthermore, many suburban communities are closely split between the two parties (Dover 2005, 61). Yet the strong support that the Republican Party receives from rural communities has made it a leading champion of rural concerns in state politics. Conversely, the Democratic Party's strong urban base has made it particularly attentive to urban concerns. As the parties grew increasingly divided along these rural-urban lines in the 1980s, the two sides eventually exploded into conflict, generating some of the state's most intense battles in the legislature and over ballot initiatives. The political conflict between rural and urban Oregon that we see today represents a continuation of those battles. To understand the impact of the rural and urban divide on Oregon politics, it is important to look at how the divide has become drawn along partisan lines.

A partisan realignment

Over the past decade, many political scientists have argued that the nation has gone through a realignment of the major political parties that is at least in part based along rural and urban lines. Looking at trends in congressional elections, Stonecash et al. (2003) wrote:

> The parties now differ significantly in terms of the types of districts that they represent … Increasingly, Democratic candidates win in districts that are low income, have a relatively high percentage of non-whites, and are urban. Republicans now dominate elections that are relatively affluent, white, and rural or suburban. (28).

This realignment of voters nationwide is generally considered to have started in the 1960s, as many Democrats began to split their vote to support Republican presidential candidates. The election of Ronald Reagan as president in 1980 further divided voters. Pushing a clear conservative agenda, Reagan appealed to many Americans who had grown disillusioned with government in the post-Vietnam and Watergate era, drawing them into the Republican Party. With Reagan and the Republican Party championing lower taxes, reduced government spending, and a stronger military, the Democratic Party responded by offering economic and social programs that appealed to more liberal voters. Prior to these events, the Republican and Democratic Parties both appealed to a broad spectrum of voters on the left and the right. As the two parties began to present voters with distinctive policy choices in the 1980s, however, support for them began to change, generating the new partisan alignment (Abramowitz and Saunders 2006, 177).

Oregon has gone through a similar realignment, one that is based heavily along rural-urban lines. The presence of this realignment can be seen by examining party registration in rural and urban areas of the state over time. To do this, we divided the state into seven regions that differ in the extent to which they are urbanized. Using this categorization gives a more precise picture of the changes in the state than simply dividing the state into rural and urban areas. We then examined the registration figures for the two major political parties in each of these regions since 1968, two years after Tom McCall was elected governor and the golden era of Oregon politics is often considered to have begun. The seven regions are:

Eastern Oregon.[3] Despite its growing service sector, especially in tourism, this area remains heavily dependent on agriculture and natural-resource extraction. Although population trends are highly variable here, with Bend a notable area of growth, the region represents the most rural part of the state (Crandall and Weber 2005).

Southern Oregon.[4] These western Oregon counties resemble those of eastern Oregon in their strong dependence on natural-resource production, especially timber, and in the dominance of conservative cultural values. The significant influx of retirees, in the area around Ashland and Medford in particular, and the steep decline of timber production have moved the economy toward greater reliance on service activities. In general the region remains predominantly rural.

Mid-Willamette Valley.[5] This area combines a strong agricultural sector with a legacy of industrial development and an increasingly strong service sector, especially in the Salem area. Except for Salem, communities remain identified with agricultural and natural-resource activities with some centers of industrial employment. Many areas within the Mid-Willamette Valley retain a rural character, but with the presence of Salem—the state's second largest city—the region is less rural than are eastern and southern Oregon.

The North Coast. This region is complex, characterized by a strong former reliance on natural resources and agriculture that is slowly giving way to service-sector activities, particularly tourism. Although some measures depict it as rural, the region's dependence on tourism and the presence of many retirement and vacation residents give it a different character from other rural regions of the state.[6] It includes Columbia County, which has become a bedroom community of the Portland metropolitan area (Vander Vliet 2003).

Portland suburbs. Despite sharing in Portland's economy, Washington and Clackamas counties have distinct differences from Portland and are less urban than Portland and Multnomah County.

University counties. Benton County and Lane County are distinctive as the homes of Oregon State University and the University of Oregon, respectively. Although Lane County in particular has a significant agricultural and industrial sector, overall this region is dominated by education, research, high-tech industry, and other spin-off activities that are largely categorized as service.

Multnomah County. Dominated by Portland, this region embodies both the economic and social characteristics associated with postindustrial society. Services dominate the economy, while economic change and growth are driven by globalized industries.

Partisan registration for all seven regions was fairly even in the 1960s (table 6), with the Democratic Party maintaining an advantage everywhere, and trending upward in all seven areas before peaking in the late 1970s. After reaching that peak, the figures began to diverge by region. Over the next two decades the eastern and southern counties grew increasingly Republican, while Multnomah County remained strongly Democratic. The other regions also saw a decline in support for the Democratic Party after 1976, though not to the same degree as in eastern and southern Oregon. In short, the table shows that the most rural parts of the state have grown increasingly Republican, while the most urban area—Multnomah County—has maintained a strong Democratic advantage. The partisan trends in other regions of the state fall in between these extremes, with the mid-Willamette counties gaining a Republican edge and the north coast and university counties maintaining a sizable Democratic majority, though not to the same extent as in Multnomah County. These patterns in voter registration tell us that the

	Eastern Oregon	Southern Oregon	Mid-Willamette	North Coast	Portland Suburbs	University Counties	Multnomah County
1968	56	56	50	60	51	55	60
1972	58	58	54	63	54	60	64
1976	59	61	57	66	57	63	67
1980	56	58	55	64	54	59	64
1984	54	55	53	63	52	59	65
1988	52	53	52	62	50	58	64
1992	51	52	51	62	50	59	65
1996	47	48	48	59	48	57	65
2000	45	47	47	58	48	56	67
2004	42	44	46	57	49	57	69
2008	44	47	49	60	55	63	77

Table 6. Democrats as percentage of major party registration, 1968-2008. Source: Oregon Secretary of State, Official Voter Registration and Turnout Statistics.

state went through a partisan realignment based on the rural-urban divide beginning in the early 1980s. It is interesting to note, however, that all regions experienced gains in Democratic Party registration in 2008. The meaning of this recent change is a topic we will take up in the conclusion.

While voters have become more sharply divided along party lines, they have also come to identify more strongly with their party's ideology. The result is that partisan affiliation is far more important in shaping politics today than it was in the so-called golden era of Oregon politics. Recent research on the American electorate as a whole has found that voters have become more ideologically coherent in their policy preferences and are more likely to identify with the political parties based on their ideological positions. As a result of these trends, American political parties are not only divided along rural and urban lines but along ideological ones as well (Abramowitz and Saunders 2006). Thus the partisan polarization we see in the nation reflects profound ideological differences that now exist within the electorate. The Republican Party has emerged with an ideologically conservative rural base, while the Democratic Party has a strong ideologically liberal, urban one. Given the economic, social, and technological trends that have reshaped Oregon, there is no reason to believe that Oregon voters are any different from those in the rest of the country in being divided by ideological, partisan, and rural-urban lines.

The regional conflict in governance

In the early 1990s, as the Oregon electorate grew further apart along all these regional lines, the polarization finally exploded in the functioning of the state government. While there were some earlier clashes between rural and urban areas, several key events beginning in 1990 brought the regional conflict to a head.

The first was the June 26, 1990, decision by the U. S. Fish and Wildlife Service (USFWS) to list the northern spotted owl as a threatened species under the provisions of the Endangered Species Act of 1973. The listing forced the federal government to severely restrict timber harvesting on federal land, and it also required private landowners to take steps to avoid harming the owls (Meyers 1991).

At the time of the listing, the federal government was channeling 25 percent of federal timber receipts to county governments, which helped pay for a large share of the counties' activities (Pytte 1990). The loss of both jobs and federal assistance would leave local governments floundering. Prior to the listing, there had been simmering disagreement between rural and urban areas over land-use and environmental regulations, but the listing galvanized rural residents over what they saw as a threat to their communities and livelihood. The battle sparked by the spotted owl quickly grew beyond just a concern over saving jobs into a conflict over many related issues revolving around land use and government regulation. The anger in rural communities led to the formation of a coalition of groups that sought to protect access to public lands for commercial uses and to promote private-property rights. Composed of groups representing timber, farming, ranching, mining, and property-rights advocates, the seventy-seven-thousand-member Oregon Lands Coalition soon became a leading player in promoting the economic and conservation values of rural communities (Durbin 1992).

A few months after the listing, another issue arose in a different policy realm. On November 6, 1990, state voters passed Measure 5, an initiative petition that limited property taxes and required the state to compensate local school districts for lost revenue. Taxes and school funding have long been important in Oregon politics, but Measure 5 intensified the conflict over these issues, while making it more difficult for the state to balance its budget. The battles related to Measure 5 immediately began to be drawn along rural-urban lines, whether the issues were over school funding or raising state revenue to balance the budget (Church 1993).

A final event that occurred in 1990 and helped increase the regional conflict was that the Republican Party gained control of the state House of Representatives for the first time since the 1971 session, giving rural communities a greater voice in state affairs—though with the Democrats in control of the Senate, neither party could control the legislature's output. The big issue confronting the legislature in the 1991 session was how it was going to respond to the financial changes produced by the passage of Measure 5. The geographical divide made it difficult for the legislature to find consensus on that and other issues (Mapes 1991; Mapes and Hill 1991). As the session wore on, it became clear how important the rural-urban split had become in state politics: "The split between the two Oregons has always been around, but Measure 5 and the transfer of power to Republicans in the House have strengthened the rifts" (Mapes 1991).

A new area of conflict opened up in 1992, this one over cultural and moral values. The 1992 election included Measure 9, an initiative petition that would have limited civil-rights protections for homosexuals and prohibited Oregon governments from "promoting" homosexuality. In the preceding election, the

Oregon Citizens Alliance (OCA) had sponsored two anti-abortion initiatives that had galvanized the opposing views of rural and urban areas, yet Measure 9 brought the divide over moral questions to an entirely new level. Led by Lon Mabon and the OCA, the effort to restrict the rights of homosexuals became a "thunderous crusade" for social conservatives (*The Oregonian* 1992, 1993a). Although the battle was not drawn solely along rural-urban lines, the state was heavily divided by region, with rural voters strongly supporting the initiative and urban voters opposing it (Meehan 1992).

As these events played out, the battle between the regions began to reach into the operation of state government. While the 1991 legislative session had some conflict, the ability of the two sides to find common ground fell apart in 1993, with the opposing sides repeatedly lined up along partisan and regional lines in one major policy debate after another. On one side was the Republican House majority, which was supporting rural positions; on the other was the Senate Democratic majority, which was supporting urban ones. The legislature finally adjourned in August; the policy battles had forced it to remain in session for a record number of days (Kiyomura 1993; *The Oregonian* 1993b).

The partisan conflict in the 1993 session was so intense that it is often considered a turning point for governance in Oregon from which the state has never recovered (*Bend Bulletin* 2006; Sadler 2005). At the heart of the conflict were the profound ideological and value differences between parties, differences that were a product of the state's rural and urban divide. While the harsh political battles seen in Oregon today are often blamed on partisan politics, the real cause of the turmoil has remained these ideological and value differences between the rural and urban parts of the state.

Support for Public Policy

The one question that remains to be answered is: How deep and wide is this divide? Just how does the rural/urban split actually shape the public's attitude to different public policies? In this final section, we examine voters' opinions on a variety of issues to determine the extent to which the divide affects public policy. Our concern is whether the economic and social forces associated with the postindustrial economy act as a wedge in a wide range of policy areas and whether there are areas where it might be possible to build consensus.

We explored how residents of each of our seven regions voted on certain ballot measures in this decade and in the early 1990s. We decided to look at ballot measures because these votes provide a direct measure of public opin-ion on specific policy proposals. We chose measures dealing with four policy areas: fiscal matters, health and education, the environment, and cultural or moral issues. The measures are summarized in the Appendix to this chapter.

We looked at voting during two periods (1990-1996 and 2000-2007) with the goal of determining whether political values have shifted in response to the profound shift in Oregon's economy during the past decade. Our focus was not on which measures passed, or even the margins by which they passed or failed, but on detecting regional patterns in voters' opinions on public-policy questions. More specifically, our analysis considers the extent to which people in the different regions hold postmaterialistic values, which, as we have seen, are more often associated with liberal than with conservative policy preferences. In essence, we are comparing the liberal and conservative character of each region, because we believe the convergence, or divergence, of voters' values across the regions is particularly important in understanding how deeply the state is divided. If the state is indeed split by the rise of the postindustrial society, and the other trends described above, then we would expect to find the following:

Fiscal policy. Post-industrial economies are marked by investment in social infrastructures, particularly in human capital such as education. The willing-ness of residents in postindustrial economies to invest in such infrastructure, combined with their greater identification with such postmaterialist values as equity and quality of life, implies greater support for government taxation and spending in these communities. Residents of areas whose economy is based on agriculture, natural-resource extraction, and industry, on the other hand, would be expected to favor fiscal conservatism and smaller govern-ment, since they are generally more concerned about basic material needs and generally perceive that economic success is related primarily to labor and private investment. In other words, we would expect to find more support for taxes and spending in the more urban areas, and less in rural ones. We looked at two tax and revenue measures from the mid-1990s, Measure 5 in 1994 and Measure 25 in 1996. For the first decade of the twenty-first century we examined two tax measures, 30 (2004) and 41 (2006), and one limiting government spending, Measure 48 (2006).

Education and health care. Ballot-measure voting on education and health-care policy provides another perspective on voter attitudes toward the proper role of government. We would expect the rural regions of the state, being more conservative, to be generally opposed to government spending and direct government involvement in education and health care, while urban areas should be more supportive of government spending. For the 1990s we examined the voting on school vouchers, Measure 11 (1990), and a proposed increase in tobacco taxes, Measure 44 (1996). For the 2000s, we looked at measures focusing on education (Measure 19 in 2002), health care (Measure 23 in 2002), and a tobacco tax (Measure 50 in 2007).

Environmental issues. Voting on environmental issues is a frequently used measure of postmaterialist values. Environmental concern represents higher-order needs or values beyond those of subsistence, economic growth, and health and safety. For these reasons, it is likely that the more urban counties would disproportionately favor environmental policies, while the more rural communities of eastern and southern Oregon would oppose them. For the 1990s, we looked at measures dealing with recycling (Measure 6 in 1990), salmon harvests (Measure 8 in 1992), mining rules (Measure 14 in 1994), and cougar hunting (Measure 18 in 1994). For the 2000s, we looked at measures involving timber production in state forests (Measure 34 in 2004) and property rights (Measure 37 in 2004 and Measure 50 in 2007). Together these represented a wide cross-section of environmental and land-use issues.

Cultural issues. As noted earlier, the postindustrial economy and contemporary urbanization are commonly associated with new perspectives on personal freedoms such as women's rights, gay rights, and abortion. The materialist value systems more prevalent in the less wealthy and generally less urbanized areas may be linked to a more deferential or supportive attitude towards authority and tradition than that found in postindustrial societies (Inglehart and Baker 2000). The closeness of agricultural and natural-resource dependent communities and the desire to prevent the erosion of their sense of community may also lead to support for traditional conservative cultural values. For the 1990s, we looked at the 1990 anti-abortion measures, 8 and 10; Measure 9, restricting the civil rights of homosexuals, in 1992; and two 1994 measures, physician-assisted suicide (Measure 16) and restriction on speech regarding pornography (Measure 19). For the 2000s, we looked at the vote on gay marriage (Measure 36 in 2004) and on parental notification for abortions (Measure 43 in 2006).

The results of the analysis are shown in table 7. For consistency, the table shows the average voting percentage for the more conservative positions. The voting pattern across all four issue areas and in both time periods is consistent

	Fiscal issues		Education, health		Environment		Cultural issues	
	1990s	2000s	1990s	2000s	1990s	2000s	1990s	2000s
Eastern	52.9	45.2	43.9	66.3	69.0	63.8	47.1	63.1
Southern	52.6	44.5	44.5	65.6	64.5	66.1	48.6	60.3
Mid-Willamette	53.2	45.8	42.0	62.2	60.2	57.2	49.0	60.3
North Coast	52.4	42.8	39.8	60.7	58.2	57.2	44.9	50.7
Portland suburbs	51.6	44.9	34.9	58.4	51.3	52.3	43.0	51.4
University counties	41.8	33.7	32.1	54.9	55.9	49.0	40.0	42.9
Multnomah	43.9	35.8	35.2	49.3	45.4	39.8	39.2	34.9
County average	49.8	41.8	41.9	63.6	63.8	60.5	46.4	58.5

Table 7. Oregon voting in four policy areas, 1990s and 2000s (percent of conservative vote by county).

with the picture we have drawn of the state: The most rural parts of the state—eastern and southern Oregon—tend to be the most conservative. The mid-Willamette Valley also tends to vote more conservatively. On the other hand, the state's most urban region—Multnomah County—tends to be the most liberal, with the university counties following close behind.

As predicted, education and health measures received stronger support from the more urban areas of the state, especially Multnomah County and the university counties. The eastern and southern counties oppose environmental regulations much more strongly than any other parts of the state, while the other counties that depend significantly on agriculture and resource production consistently oppose environmental regulations, though less strongly. Voting on education, health, and environmental measures indicates the divided nature of the state's economic base, with postindustrial areas viewing government much more favorably. On cultural issues, the rural counties consistently vote in a far more conservative pattern than the Portland metropolitan area and the university counties. The most interesting aspect of this pattern is that the different regions of the state appear to be drifting further apart on cultural issues. A convergence of cultural values is not likely until this trend reverses, although Portland's cultural liberalism is spreading into the suburbs.

Voting patterns on fiscal issues offer one of the few exceptions to our expectations. In particular, the Portland suburbs were more closely aligned with the rural regions of the state than with Multnomah County or the university counties. The very consistent 10-point-greater support for taxes in Multnomah and the university counties reflects stronger support for the programs associated with government spending and greater acceptance of governmental activism.

One partial explanation for the fiscal conservatism of suburban counties may be that they still have significant rural areas, but a more powerful explanation is that suburban residents retain a concern for economic growth associated with industrial society. As a result, they perceive government as a threat to individual economic autonomy and the private-investment model of wealth creation and personal satisfaction. Battles to control the suburbs have marked the American political scene for the past decade, with business-oriented conservatism having the edge until recent elections, when the Republican Party's emphasis on cultural issues appears to have eroded its suburban power.[7] President Obama's recent Democratic regulatory activism, tax proposals, and health care plan may enable Republicans to reconnect with suburban voters' pro-business concerns once again. The November 2010 election indicates the importance of the complex nature of suburban districts. While Democratic gubernatorial candidate John Kitzhaber won a plurality with more than 49 percent of the vote in Washington County, he received just over 44 percent in the more-rural suburban county of Clackamas.

The results from this voting analysis reveal two key characteristics about the state. The first is that the regional divide in the state clearly reflects differences in economic bases, and the accompanying trends of urbanization, globalization, technological development, and evolving environmental values. The consistency of these findings makes us confident that the divergent rise of the postindustrial society explains a great deal of why Oregon is divided along regional lines. The second is that the state has gone through a partisan realignment that is also ideological in character. The more rural parts of the state are not only Republican but consistently hold conservative policy preferences on a wide range of issues. The urban parts of the state are not only Democratic, but their residents hold liberal policy preferences.

Toward a More Unified Oregon?

Can the divide between rural and urban Oregon be bridged? These findings indicate that it will be hard to discover common ground between Oregon's rural and urban areas given the divergent economic, social, ideological, and partisan values. It will be very difficult for state and local government officials to come up with solutions to the state's most pressing policy concerns that are politically acceptable to both rural and urban areas. Yet even within these findings, one can see glimmers of hope.

First, as we have made clear throughout this chapter, the state has been going through significant economic, social, and technological changes that have contributed to the political divide. Over time, it is quite likely that Oregon will see new developments that may help diminish this divide. For example, the rise of universal wide-band Internet access reduces the difficulties of moving postindustrial economic activities to rural areas. Moreover, despite recent setbacks, the increasing diversity of the economy in the Bend area demonstrates a model for development that directly connects the rural areas with the global economy as more than simply a source of raw materials. While not a panacea, the development of more specialized, value-enhanced agricultural activities such as winemaking, craft brewing, and specialized crops also offers routes for closing the distance between rural and urban economies.

More than anything else, if the state government took steps to boost the economic position of the rural communities, the rural and urban areas would no longer be as divided by differences in economic well-being, which might lead to more agreement on other policy issues. On the other hand, of course, if the nation's current economic troubles continue to worsen, the regional divide may diminish as both rural and urban areas worry about their economic futures. Beyond economic change, the rural areas are likely to continue to become more ethnically diverse and better tied into new technologies. As these changes occur, the regions will become more similar. Finally, it may also help temper the conflict if the Democratic Party is able to retain, or even expand, the gains in registration it made during the 2008 election[8] (see table 6). It is hard to know what this increase in registration means and where it will lead, since it is so recent, yet it may suggest increasing ideological similarities across the regions.

There are signs that the Democratic Party has made lasting gains in the state. For one, the Republican Party was unable to capture the governor's office or any of the congressional seats in the 2010 election despite the broad success it enjoyed nationwide. In addition, there was almost no change in party registration in any of the regions since 2008. The 2010 election demonstrates that Democrats can retain statewide power in the face of contrary national trends. The continuation of their statewide supremacy may also reflect the depth of Oregon's regional division. Kitzhaber's victory in the governor's race was based on winning only six counties; by far the most important contributor to his success was the support of more than 70 percent of voters in the most populous county, Multnomah. The

Oregon House split 30-30, along the same rural-urban lines we identify here (Oregon Secretary of State 2010a). Kitzhaber will have to find a way to reach across this divide.

Second, the findings presented in table 5 provide another ray of hope. While the rural and urban areas clearly differ strongly on environmental issues, there are some areas of agreement. Of particular importance is that the respondents in both the rural and urban areas tend to agree that the "ecological crisis" facing us today has not been exaggerated. The consistency of this response across regions tells us that residents throughout the state may ultimately find some common ground on environmental matters. Of course, as long as rural areas face economic hard times, and as long as environmental policies are seen as a threat to jobs, then this may be unrealistic. However, if the state can find common ground on environmental matters—one of the areas in which the regions are most divided—it would raise hope that it could be found elsewhere.

Finally, on fiscal issues, the election results shown in table 7 reveal that the divide between the most rural and urban parts of the state on economic matters is not nearly as wide as it is on many other policy matters. The votes indicate that there is some agreement across the state on broad rules governing revenue and spending. Moreover, when one looks at the vote on some specific measures, rather than the averages shown in table 7, there are additional areas in which the rural and urban parts of the state agree. For example, in the 1990s, eastern and southern Oregon residents voted as consistently against school vouchers as did those in Multnomah County. The cross-regional agreement on these issues suggests that the state may be able to find common ground on some specific spending and revenue policies, especially in broad educational and social programs, or on policy matters that do not squarely fit into the ideological divide.

However, given the different economic and social problems confronted by rural and urban communities, one should not expect state policies and programs to succeed if they treat rural and urban regions the same. Statewide policies on revenue and expenditures may find more acceptability if there are significant elements of local control.

Despite these glimmers of hope, finding common ground may be difficult for some time. Clearly, the wide split in the state on cultural issues suggests that the regional division on these types of issues shows no signs of moderating. Moreover, the continued chasm on environmental matters seems just as unlikely to end, despite the agreement in some of the survey questions we discussed. The state is likely to function more efficiently if it continues to see unified partisan control of the legislature and governor's office, but having unified control does nothing to end the regional divide. The problem confronting the state, as one columnist wrote recently, is that the rural-urban split "isn't simply political, open to split-the-difference deal-making. It's driven by basic values differences, on land and lifestyle issues . . . steel traps and gay rights" (Sarasohn 2001).

As long as Oregon is divided by different values and ideologies, it will be difficult to find agreement on major policy issues. Agreement will be reached only when the political values and ideologies held by Oregonians become more alike, or, alternatively, less all encompassing. Given the vast economic and social differences across the state that we have described, it seems unlikely that rural and urban residents will soon become more ideologically alike. Thus perhaps the only way in which the state will find agreement is if it can move some policy debates outside the normal political discourse, so that they are isolated from the ideological conflict that has come to define Oregon politics in recent decades. To many Oregonians, the state confronts a variety of problems that need to be solved, from inadequate health care to poor education to fiscal instability. While the rural and urban divide may make it difficult to address these issues, it does not make it impossible to do so if state residents can put aside their disagreements on social values to resolve shared problems. While it may seem simple to focus on the concerns shared by rural and urban Oregonians, the state's political divide makes cooperation a relentlessly difficult challenge.

Appendix: Ballot Measures Demonstrating Oregon Policy Voting

Fiscal measures

- Measure 5 (1994). Require a public vote on all tax and fee increases. Rejected with 44.7 percent "Yes" votes.
- Measure 25 (1996). Require a three-fifths majority for the legislature to pass any taxes. Passed with 54.7 percent "Yes" votes.
- Measure 30 (2004). Overturn temporary tax increase to replace lost revenues due to economic downturn. Passed with 59 percent "Yes" votes.

- Measure 41 (2006). Cut taxes by allowing full deduction of federal income taxes on state taxable income. Rejected with 37.1 percent "Yes" votes.
- Measure 48 (2006). Hold growth of state spending to growth of the economy. Rejected with 29.1 percent "Yes" votes.

Health and Education Measures

- Measure 11 (1990). Create school vouchers. Rejected with 42.2 percent "Yes" votes.
- Measure 44 (1996). Create a 25-cent-per-pack tax on cigarettes with revenues to be spent on health-care programs. Passed with 55.5 percent "Yes" votes.
- Measure 19 (2002). Use school stability fund principle to support K-12 education immediately and set up provisions for future fund support. Passed with 51.9 percent "Yes" votes.
- Measure 23 (2002). Establish universal health-care system with new taxes. Rejected with 21.5 "Yes" votes.
- Measure 50 (2007). Create an 87-cent-per-pack tax on cigarettes and other tobacco products. Rejected with 40.7 percent "Yes" votes.

Environmental Measures

- Measure 6 (1990). Require material to be recyclable. Rejected with 32.3 percent "Yes" votes.
- Measure 8 (1992). Restrict salmon-fishing techniques in the Columbia River. Rejected with 41 percent "Yes" votes.
- Measure 14 (1994). Create more restrictive regulations over mining activities. Rejected with 42.4 percent "Yes" votes.
- Measure 18 (1994). Strictly regulate bear and cougar hunting. Passed with 51.8 percent "Yes" votes.
- Measure 34 (2004). Restrict timber harvests on state forestlands. Rejected with 38.3 percent "Yes" votes.
- Measure 37 (2004). Protect property rights by requiring states to compensate regulatory takings. Passed with 60.6 percent "Yes" votes.
- Measure 50 (2007). Reform regulatory takings laws to support state land-use regulations. Passed with 62.1 percent "Yes" votes.

Cultural-issue Measures

- Measure 8 (1990). Restrict abortion. Rejected with 32.3 percent "Yes" votes.
- Measure 10 (1990). Require parental notice for minors seeking abortion. Rejected with 47.9 percent "Yes" votes.
- Measure 9 (1992). Forbid state from facilitating, and require state to discourage, homosexuality. Rejected with 43.5 percent "Yes" votes.
- Measure 16 (1994). Allow physician-assisted suicide. Passed with 51.8 percent "Yes" votes.
- Measure 19 (1994). Exclude obscenity and pornography from constitutional protections under state constitution. Rejected with 45.7 percent "Yes" votes.
- Measure 36 (2004). Require that a marriage be only between a man and a woman. Passed with 56.6 percent "Yes" votes.
- Measure 43 (2006). Require parental notice for minors seeking abortion. Rejected with 45.2 percent "Yes" votes.

Bibliography

Abramowitz, Alan I., and Kyle L. Saunders. 2006. "Exploring the bases of partisanship in the American electorate: Social identity vs. ideology." *Political Research Quarterly* 59: 175-87.

Bates, Tom, and Doug Bates. 1996. "Country: Portland dominance chafes like a worn saddle blanket." *The Oregonian*, Feb. 4, 1996, C4.

Beale, Calvin L., and Glen V. Fuguitt. 1990. "Decade of pessimistic nonmetro population trends ends on optimistic note." *Rural Development Perspectives* 6: 14-18.

Bell, Daniel. 1973. *The Coming of Post-industrial Society*. New York: Basic Books.

Bellah, Robert. 1985. *Habits of the Heart: Individualism and Commitment in American Life*. New York: Harper and Row.

The Bend Bulletin. "Influential Citizens." Sept. 28, 2006. http://www.bendbulletin.com/apps/pbcs.dll/article?AID=/20060928/NEWS0107/609280340. Accessed on November 4, 2010.

Bodine, Harry. 1993. "Still larger than life." *The Oregonian,* Jan. 24, 1993, Forum.

Carroll, Matthew S. 1995. *Community and the Northwestern Logger: Continuities and Changes in the Era of the Spotted Owl*. Boulder, Colo.: Westview Press.

Church, Foster. 1993. "Country consequences: The other Oregon." *The Oregonian*, July 11, 1993, A1.

Clucas, Richard A., Mark Henkels, and Brent S. Steel, eds. 2005. *Oregon Politics and Government: Progressives versus Conservative Populists*. Lincoln: University of Nebraska Press.

Crandall, Mindy, and Bruce Weber. 2005. "Defining rural Oregon: An exploration." *Rural Studies Paper Series*, RSP 05-03, November 2005. Corvallis: Oregon State University.

Dalton, Russell. 2009. *The Good Citizen: How a Younger Generation Is Reshaping American Politics*. Washington, D.C.: CQ Press.

Deavers, Kenneth L. 1989 (personal communication). "Rural development in the 1990s: Data and research." Paper presented at the Rural Social Science Symposium, American Agricultural Economics Association, Baton Rouge, Louisiana.

Dietrich, William. 1992. *The Final Forest: The Battle for the Last Great Trees of the Pacific Northwest*. New York: Simon and Schuster.

Dodds, Gordon B. 1977. *Oregon: A Bicentennial History*. New York: W. W. Norton.

Dover, E. D. 2005. "Parties and elections." In Richard A. Clucas, Mark Henkels, and Brent S. Steel, eds., *Oregon Politics and Government: Progressives versus Conservative Populists*. Lincoln: University of Nebraska Press.

Dunlap, Riley E., and Angela G. Mertig. 1992. "The evolution of the U.S. environmental movement from 1970 to 1990: An overview." In Riley E. Dunlap and Angela G. Mertig, eds., *American Environmentalism: The U.S. Environmental Movement 1970-1990*. Philadelphia: Taylor and Francis Publishers.

Dunlap, Riley E., Kent D. Van Liere, Angela G. Mertig, and Robert E. Jones. 2000. "Measuring endorsement of the new ecological paradigm: A revised NEP scale." *Journal of Social Issues* 56: 425-42.

Durbin, Kathie. 1992. "Lands coalition leads fight for timber jobs." *The Oregonian*, Jan. 27, 1992, B1.

Inglehart, Ronald. 1977. *The Silent Revolution: Changing Values and Political Styles among Western Publics*. Princeton: Princeton University Press.

Inglehart, Ronald. 1990. *Culture Shift in Advanced Industrial Society*. Princeton: Princeton University Press.

Inglehart, Ronald. 1997. *Modernization and Postmodernization: Cultural, Economic, and Political Change in 43 Societies*. Princeton: Princeton University Press.

Inglehart, Ronald, and Wayne Baker. 2000. "Modernization, cultural change, and the persistence of traditional values." *American Sociological Review* 65: 19-51.

Inglehart, Ronald, and Christian Weizel. 2010. "Changing mass priorities: The link between modernization and democracy." *Reflections* 8 (June): 551-67.

Kemp, Roger L. 2001. "Cities in the 21st century: The forces of change." *Local Focus*, League of Oregon Cities, February and April.

Kiyomura, Cathy. 1993. "Session Called a Success." *The Oregonian*, Aug. 6, 1993, A1.

Knoder, Erik A. 2005. "Summer Industries—Fishing and Tourism." Oregon Employment Department, September 2, 2005. http://www.qualityinfo.org/olmisj/ArticleReader?itemid=00004473. Accessed Oct. 28, 2008.

Mapes, Jeff. 1991. "Rural-urban split looms at session." *The Oregonian*, Feb. 10, 1991, D11.

Mapes, Jeff, and Gail Kinsey Hill. 1991. "Measure 5 set tone for 1991 legislative session." *The Oregonian*, July 1, 1991.

Mapes, Jeff. 2006. "Republican Party can't win for losing old image in Oregon." March 26, 2006, p. A 01.

Mapstats. http://www.fedstats.gov/qf/states/41000.html and http://www.fedstats.gov/qf/states/41/4159000.html. Accessed April 2007.

Maslow, Abraham. 1959. *New Knowledge in Human Values*. New York: Harper and Row.

McKee, Seth C. 2008. "Rural voters and the polarization of American presidential elections." *PS 41*: 101-108.

Meehan, Brian T. 1992. "Measure 9 reveals deep splits among Oregon voters." *The Oregonian*, Nov. 5, 1992, A1.

Meyers, Gary D. 1991. "Old-growth forests, the owl, and yew: Environmental ethics versus traditional dispute resolution." *Boston College Environmental Affairs Law Review* 18: 623-68.

Milbrath, Lester W. 1996. *Learning to Think Environmentally While There Is Still Time.* Albany, N.Y.: State University of New York Press.

Mossberger, Karen, Caroline J. Tolbert, and Mary Stansbury. 2003. *Virtual Inequality: Beyond the Digital Divide.* Washington, D.C.: Georgetown University Press.

Northwest Area Foundation. County data for Oregon. http://www.indicators.nwaf.org/DrawRegion.aspx?RegionID=41000&IndicatorID=5. Accessed Oct. 25, 2008.

Offe, Claus. 1985. "New social movements: Challenging the boundaries of institutional politics." *Social Research* 52: 817–68.

Oregon Economic and Community Development Department. http://www.oregon4biz.com/data.htm. Accessed March 27, 2009.

Oregon Office of Economic Analysis. 2007. Oregon economic forecast. March 1, 2007. http://www.oregon.gov/DAS/OEA/economic.shtml#Most_Recent_Forecast. Accessed April 2007.

Oregon Secretary of State, Elections Division. 2010a. Unofficial results of November 2, 2010, General Election. Accessed November 6, 2010. http://egov.sos.state.or.us/division/elections/results/2010G/index.html

Oregon Secretary of State, Elections Division. 2010b. Voter registration by county, September 2010. http://www.sos.state.or.us/elections/votreg/sep10.pdf. Accessed Nov. 5, 2010.

The Oregonian. 1992. "Election brings turning point to Oregon." November 8, 1992, C1.

The Oregonian. 1993a. "Rural Oregon confronts new reality." June 11, 1993, A1.

The Oregonian. 1993b. "Partisan politics commands the state." July 25, 1993, C1.

Pew Hispanic Center. 2008. "Latinos account for half of U.S. population growth since 2000." http://pewhispanic.org/reports/report.php?ReportID=96#OtherTitle. County appendix, Oct. 23, 2008. Accessed October 24, 2008.

Pytte, A. 1990. "Timber, spotted owl interests find middle ground elusive." *Congressional Quarterly Weekly Report,* September, 29, 1990: 3104-7.

Rainie, Lee, John Horrigan, and Michael Cornfield. Pew Internet and American Life Project. The Internet and Campaign 2004. http://www.pewinternet.org/Reports/2005/The-Internet-and-Campaign-2004.aspx.

Read, Richard. 2010. OregonLive.com. "Six Rural Oregon Counties See Unemployment Rise above 15 Percent in September." http://www.oregonlive.com/business/index.ssf/2010/10/unemployment_in_oregons_two_ha.html. Accessed October 31, 2010.

Sadler, Russell. 2005. "Our Childish Legislature." www.BlueOregon.com, Aug. 7, 2005. http://www.blueoregon.com/2005/08/our_childish_le.h. Accessed on November 4, 2010.

Sarasohn, David. 2001. "Politics on both sides of our great divide." *The Oregonian,* Jan. 7, 2001, Forum.

Scott, James K. 2005. "Assessing the quality of municipal government web sites." *State and Local Government Review* 37: 151-65.

Simon, Christopher, Brent S. Steel, and Nicholas P. Lovrich. 2011. *State and Local Government: Sustainability in the 21st Century.* Oxford: Oxford University Press.

Steger, Mary Ann, John C. Pierce, Brent S. Steel, and Nicholas P. Lovrich. 1989. "Political culture, post-material values, and the new environmental paradigm: A comparative analysis of Canada and the United States." *Political Behavior* 11: 233-54.

Stonecash, Jeff, Mark Brewer, and Mack Mariani. 2003. *Diverging Parties: Realignment, Social Change, and Political Polarization.* Boulder, Colo.: Westview Press.

U.S. Bureau of the Census. Urban and rural population by state: 1990 and 2000. http://www.census.gov/compendia/statab/tables/08s0029.pdf. Accessed October 17, 2008.

Vander Vliet, Amy. 2003. "Commuting patterns within the Portland PMSA." Oregon Employment Department, June 30, 2003. http://www.qualityinfo.org/olmisj/ArticleReader?itemid=00003071. Accessed October 28, 2008.

Winograd, Morley, and Michael Hais. 2009. *Millennial Makeover: MySpace, YouTube, and the Future of American Politics.* New Brunswick, N.J.: Rutgers University Press.

Yohannan, Jason J. 2005. "Eastern Oregon: Service workers dominate occupational landscape." Oregon Employment Department, December 6, 2005. http://www.qualityinfo.org/olmisj/ArticleReader?itemid=00004669. Accessed October 17, 2008.

Chapter 8
Critical Linkages
Strengthening Clusters in Urban and Rural Oregon

Sheila Martin

Introduction

People living in the urban and rural parts of our state are linked in a number of ways. First, they are linked through relationships developed through migration. Migration has occurred in both directions: from the rural areas to urban areas for the purposes of education, work, and social interaction, and from urban to rural areas to retire or simply to find an alternative way of life (Hammer 2008).

Urban and rural Oregonians are also linked through trade in goods and services. As demonstrated in Chapter 5, almost $7.4 billion in goods and services purchased by the periphery comes from the core area of Oregon, while the core purchases $1.8 billion in goods and services from the periphery. As was documented in Chapter 6, urban and rural Oregonians are also linked by the state's revenue-sharing system that is used to equalize the services available for the citizens of its state, especially for education and health care. This linkage is critical, because it means that economic vitality in one part of the state provides benefits to citizens in other parts. In effect, we all benefit from economic success in one part of the state because state tax revenues are shared statewide. Finally, urban and rural Oregonians are united by a state boundary and a government that ensures that decisions made in Salem affect all parts of our state.

Oregonians are also connected through their business relationships, which link the urban and rural economies in fundamental ways. Earlier in our state's history this economic connection was obvious, because the natural resources industries were fundamental drivers of the economy in both urban and rural areas. But as other industries became more prominent, particularly in urban areas, there was a growing disconnect between the metropolitan regions of our state and the rural areas, which have in many ways been left behind in the economic boom fueled by technology industries.

While metropolitan Oregon has always had a more diversified economy than rural Oregon, many jobs in urban areas were historically tied to the natural-resources industries. The legal, financial, trade, and transportation sectors served natural resources, and a number of urban-based food and wood-processing manufacturers also depended on raw materials from the rural areas. The percentage of personal income derived directly from farming, forestry, and fishing was about 8 percent in nonmetropolitan areas in 1969; that percentage grew to over 10 percent in 1974, but then fell to about 4 percent in 1990. Statewide, the percentage of personal income derived directly from natural-resources industries also fell, from about 3 percent in 1969 to about 2 percent in 1990. But the decline in this industry was clearly felt most acutely in rural areas (figure 1).

After 1990, the state's dependence on natural resources further declined as the percentage of personal income from computer-related industries began

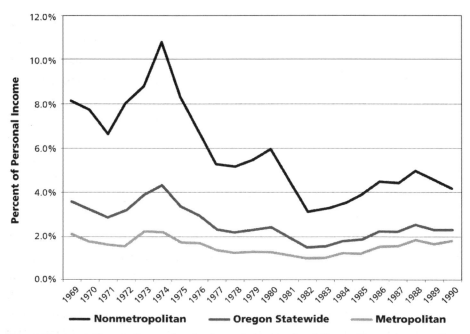

Figure 1. Percentage of personal income from farming, agricultural services, fishing, and forestry in metropolitan and nonmetropolitan areas and statewide, 1969 to 1990. Source: U.S. Bureau of Economic Analysis 2008.

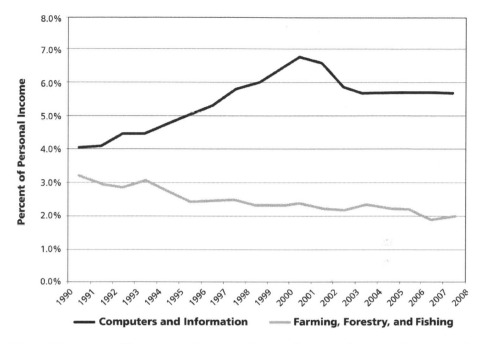

Figure 2. Percentage of Oregon statewide personal income from natural-resources industries and information industries, 1990 to 2007. Source: U.S. Bureau of Economic Analysis 2008.

to rise (figure 2). In the 1990s these two economic sectors contributed about the same amount of personal income to our state, but since then they have pulled apart. This trend has largely left the rural parts of our state behind. While the computer and electronic products industry employed approximately forty thousand workers statewide in 2007, with an average annual wage of $88,226—significantly higher than the state's average annual wage of $39,564—over 80 percent of those jobs were in the three-county Portland metropolitan area (Oregon Employment Department 2008). The sense among many rural people of economic disconnection exacerbates the division between urban and rural policymakers, as rural leaders see a generation of wealth in the cities that they and their fellow citizens largely do not share.

However, several industry clusters key to the Oregon economy span urban and rural areas and their future well-being hinges on strong relationships between urban and rural businesses, consumers, and supporting institutions. Strengthening these connections can improve the profitability of both urban and rural businesses in these industries. I will focus on two key industry clusters that have important components in both urban and rural areas: farms and food, and forest and wood products.

This discussion of industry clusters is based on the definition developed by Michael Porter (2000), who defines a cluster as "geographic concentrations of interconnected companies, specialized suppliers, service providers, firms in related industries, and associated institutions (e.g., universities, standards agencies, trade associations) in a particular field that compete but also cooperate" (15). He argues that these firms draw productive advantage from their mutual proximity and connections. The term "cluster" has become so ubiquitous in the discussion of industry specializations within regions that it is often used interchangeably with "industry" to refer to the private, public, and nonprofit organizations that in some way participate in or influence the sector.

Urban and Rural Dimension of Clusters

The food and beverage industry

Food in Oregon is a diverse and complex industry. A food-cluster study recently released by the Northwest Food Processors shows that farm production employs the largest number of people in this industry, more than one hundred thousand (Applied Development Economics 2006), closely followed

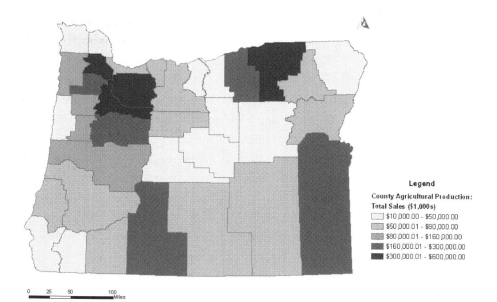

Legend

County Agricultural Production:
Total Sales ($1,000s)
- $10,000.00 - $50,000.00
- $50,000.01 - $80,000.00
- $80,000.01 - $160,000.00
- $160,000.01 - $300,000.00
- $300,000.01 - $600,000.00

0   25   50   100
                            Miles

Figure 3. Gross farm and ranch sales by county, 2007. Source: Oregon Department of Agriculture 2008.

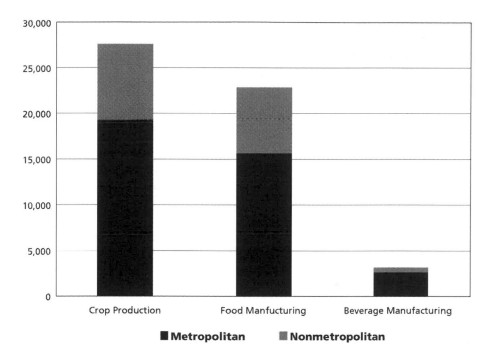

■ **Metropolitan** ■ **Nonmetropolitan**

Figure 4. Food-industry employment in metropolitan and nonmetropolitan Oregon, 2007. Source: Oregon Employment Department 2008.

by transportation and distribution of food products. Oregon's food industry is most concentrated in fruit and vegetables, and its fastest-growing segment is wineries and breweries.

The food industry is spread throughout the state and has both a rural and an urban presence: three of the four counties with the highest agricultural income are part of metropolitan areas (figure 3). In fact, over 50 percent of the value of Oregon's crop production comes from counties considered metropolitan. About 70 percent of employment in crop production and 70 percent of food-product manufacturing occurs in metropolitan counties (figure 4). Over 80 percent of employment in beverage manufacturing occurs in metropolitan counties. Thus, while agriculture and food are generally considered industries with rural ties, they clearly depend on labor from the metropolitan areas as well as raw materials from the rural parts of the state. Of course, rural areas are more dependent on agricultural products and related industries because these make up a larger share of the rural economy.

Forest and wood products

Like the food industry, the forest-products cluster in Oregon is very diverse. The core industry includes forest owners, harvesters, sawmills, secondary wood-product manufacturers, and intermediaries such as trucking companies. Related industries include equipment manufacturers and a variety of entities such as banks, insurance companies, government agencies, and nongovernmental organizations. The wood-products industry has been the main influence on the industrial development of Oregon. The metals industry, the industrial-machinery industry, and the transportation industries in Oregon all arose to serve the needs of the forest industry. It is not surprising, then, that although the wood-products industry suffered a 10 percent loss in jobs from 1990 to 2000, it is still a substantial presence, employing over eighty-five thousand people (E. D. Hovee & Co. 2005).

Employment in the wood-products sector also spans rural and urban Oregon. The growth and extraction side of the industry includes logging and forestry; these primary activities, captured by NAICS code 113 (U.S. Census Bureau), are necessarily located in the more rural areas of the state, while the secondary-products sectors—including veneer, plywood, engineered

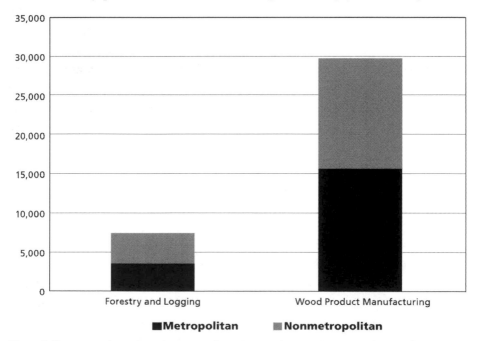

Figure 5. Forestry and wood-products manufacturing employment in metropolitan and nonmetropolitan Oregon, 2007. Source: Oregon Employment Department 2008.

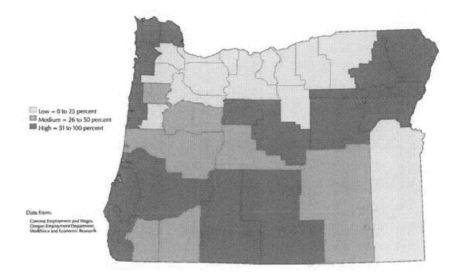

Figure 6. The forest sector as a percentage of traded-sector employment by county, 2001. Source: E. D. Hovee & Co. 2005.

wood products, and other kinds of wood-products manufacturing—are lo-cated more heavily in metropolitan areas. Sawmills, although they are part of the wood-products manufacturing industry, are often located in rural areas, closer to the source of raw material. Almost half of employment in logging and forestry occurs in counties considered part of metropolitan areas (figure 5). Wood-products manufacturing is spread across the state as well, with just a bit more than half of its employment in the metropolitan counties. The Portland three-county area accounts for about 18 percent of total industry employment (E. D. Hovee & Co. 2005), but many rural counties depend more than do urban counties on the forest sector for the majority of their traded-sector employment (figure 6).

Urban-Rural Cluster Connections

We have established that the food cluster and the forest-products cluster in-habit both urban and rural parts of the state. But how well are the urban and rural parts connected? And how can these industries benefit from a stronger connection?

Producing a final food or forest product requires the participation of a network of companies and organizations including suppliers, specialized infrastructure, markets, and marketing initiatives, to source raw materials, ship and process them, design and produce a final product, and ship it for export.

Improving outcomes for Oregon's food and forest-products industries will require improving the performance of every company that touches the product—from the farm or forest to the consumer. One approach to meeting this goal is to examine the value chain—the series of activities by which a business system creates value for a customer (Porter 1985). In this model, profit depends on creating value (defined by what a customer is willing to pay) in excess of the cost of activities within the value chain. This value is created either by reducing the costs within the value chain, or by pursuing differentiation—that is, identifying those characteristics of the product or service that distinguish it from those produced by competitors and add to its appeal to a particular target market. Differentiation increases the value of the product to the consumer and therefore the consumer's willingness to pay (Porter 1985).

A key driver of both cost and differentiation within the value chain is the quality of the linkages among activities. How smooth is the handoff of a product or service from one stage in the process to the next? This depends in large part on the interrelationships among the separate business units that comprise the value chain. Inefficient linkages can introduce transactions costs, including the cost of gathering information and searching for the product that meets your needs (search and information costs), physically obtaining the good or service (transportation costs), establishing a price (bargaining costs), and ensuring that what you receive is what was contracted for (policing and enforcement costs) (Williamson 1981).

Examining and lowering transaction costs is part of the process of improving the value chain. These costs are often lowered by making investments such as relocating production to reduce transportation costs, developing a long-term contract to reduce bargaining costs, or developing the technology and protocols for information exchange that lowers information costs (as in, for example, just-in-time inventory systems). Sometimes the investment consists simply of the time required to establish trust among partners. Once these investments are made, the partners to the transaction are more likely to continue their relationships because the investment has reduced the cost of future transactions, therefore increasing the value to the customer and increasing profit.

For natural-resources industries such as food and forest products, many of the linkages and the transactions between them occur between urban and rural entities. Thus, following Porter's logic, increasing value and profit for companies within these value chains requires smoother transitions, stronger linkages, and perhaps investments in the relationships represented by these transactions.

While it makes common sense that improving relationships between different parts of the value chain can improve business outcomes for its members, there is also empirical evidence that these linkages are important. Recent research on the performance of industry clusters has found that improving local relationships among members of the cluster—an investment in reducing transaction costs—does indeed improve the profitability of cluster members (Schmitz 2006). Further evidence from several studies has shown that rural areas with a critical mass in specific industry clusters have enjoyed better economic performance than those that do not house strong clusters (Henry and Drabenstott 1996; Gibbs and Bernat 1997). It is important for rural clusters to be tied to the nearest metropolitan area. In part, this is because many value chains involve global actors, and reaching them requires a local partner that is globally connected (Porter et al. 2004). Connections to metropolitan areas can also facilitate the development of niche markets that can be tested and refined in adjacent urban areas before taking them to the global market.

How can the Oregon food and forest industries strengthen their clusters to improve the performance of all the companies that contribute to the development of a final product? As explained below, several initiatives are under way to establish tighter relationships between the rural and urban parts of these clusters. These initiatives represent investments that will reduce transaction costs, increase value, and improve profitability in these clusters, transforming the urban-rural relationships from arm's-length, competitive, market-driven transactions to long-term relationships.

As described by Parsons (2009), a value-chain relationship is like a marriage: "Just as a strong marriage is built on honesty, integrity, trust, good transparent communication and shared power so is a strong chain" (20). By contrast, in a typical auction, for example, there is no direct communication between seller and buyer—the auctioneer communicates the relevant information. The seller cannot tailor his product to the buyer and so has lost the opportunity to add value. Using the marriage analogy, Parsons describes the auction situation as a "one night stand."

Thus, improving the health of natural-resources industries requires moving away from the arm's-length transaction and toward more lasting relationships that build honesty, integrity, and trust. These relationships allow the members of these clusters to engage in the main strategy that will build greater value for Oregon natural resources industries—differentiation.

Product Differentiation in the Food and Forest Industries

One of the most important strategies for both food and forest products is differentiation. Rather than selling in a commodity market, Oregon companies can increase their profitability by branding and marketing their products to one or more specific segments of the market that may be willing to pay a price premium. Differentiation provides the industry additional market power, and it may be an alternative to cost-cutting strategies, which have limited effectiveness in a global market that includes suppliers with much lower input costs. Differentiation requires reaching a market that values a product with specific characteristics; it also requires a mechanism for conveying information about the differences among products.

Differentiation through certification

Certification agencies play an important role in the differentiation of farm and forest products. They act as a neutral source of information to the consumer who seeks a reliable signal that the product meets a commonly accepted set of standards for quality or some other characteristic that is not easily observable. Certification of food products in Oregon is offered by two organizations, Food Alliance and Oregon Tilth. Food Alliance certifies farm and ranch operations and food packers, processors, and distributors. A Food Alliance certification is an assurance to consumers that the producer uses sustainable production and business practices such as environmental stewardship, safe and fair working conditions, and humane treatment of animals (Food Alliance 2009). Food Alliance has certified over one hundred Oregon producers of cattle, fruit, vegetables, nuts, and grain.

Oregon Tilth provides organic-certification services to growers, processors, and handlers internationally (Oregon Tilth). Oregon Tilth has certified over five hundred companies in Oregon. Certified organic food is finding a market. The U.S. Department of Agriculture reports that organic farm-gate sales in Oregon reached $88.4 million in 2007. A recent study of organic price premiums reported that they rose from 2001 to 2004, and that premiums in 2004 ranged from 9 percent above conventional produce for oranges to 78 percent for potatoes (Stevens-Garmon et al. 2007).

Certification of wood products offers the consumer a way to differentiate among forest products on the basis of characteristics such as sustainable
or fair-trade practices. The Forest Stewardship Council (FSC) certification
program accredits independent certifiers who evaluate forest-management
activities and tracking of forest products through a chain-of-custody certification. The accredited certifiers work directly with landowners and processors
to certify that the company is meeting FSC principles and applicable regional
standards. There are a number of other certification organizations, such as
the Sustainable Forestry Initiative (SFI), that follow a similar process for forest, chain-of-custody, and fiber sourcing.

Oregon forest owners, who must manage their lands according to state
forest-practices rules and federal environmental laws, are already meeting or
exceeding most FSC or SFI standards (Fletcher et al. 2002). Exceptions include
requirements for written plans, inventories, and chain-of-custody recordkeep-
ing. Fletcher et al. (2002) conclude that pursuing certification would probably
not require significant changes in practices for most Oregon forest owners.
As certification becomes a more important strategy for global market differentiation for wood products, the Oregon forest-products industry may gain
an advantage over forest owners who pursue certification in other states with
looser regulatory environments.

The Forest Stewardship Council's certification is recognized by the United
States Green Building Council (USGBC). Builders get credit toward certification of their buildings under the Leadership in Energy and Environmental
Design (LEED) Green Building Rating System. The USGBC's Living Building
Challenge program requires all wood to be either FSC-certified or reclaimed
(U.S. Green Building Council). The certification process often involves working
closely with consultants from urban areas. For example, the Cascadia chapter
of the Green Building Council, with an office in Portland, plays an important
role in educating builders and architects about certified wood products.

The evidence that certification offers market advantages in the forest-
products industry is still thin, although there are signs that the market for
certified wood is growing. A recent study found that only one-quarter of all
builders using certified lumber believed that their customers would pay a premium for certified lumber. However, builders in the western United States are
more likely than other U.S. builders to use certified lumber, and they also are
more likely to believe that a price premium is possible; 40 percent of builders
in the Northwest and 42 percent of builders in the Southwest believe that

such a premium is possible (Ganguly and Eastin 2007). The builders surveyed believe that acceptance of certified lumber by the USGBC under the LEED program has had a big impact on the market by offering the opportunity for a future price premium for forest products. Furthermore, a recent survey of builders in the Portland area indicated an increasing demand for green building, which is likely to further increase the demand for certified lumber (Allen and Potiowsky 2008). Some secondary manufacturers of wood products are using these opportunities to differentiate their products as sustainable, in part by sourcing some of their certified wood from Oregon forests.

Differentiation through direct marketing

Another differentiation strategy is to use direct marketing to develop a relationship with buyers. The USDA estimates that, in 2007, 6,274 Oregon farms sold over $56 million worth of produce directly to customers. That represents about 16 percent of all the farms in Oregon, compared to about 6 percent of farms nationwide (USDA 2007). The value of agricultural products sold directly to individuals has steadily increased since 1992 (Martin et al. 2008). Farmers engaged in direct marketing understand the value of developing relationships with their customers. With conventional marketing, they capture only about 24 percent of the retail price of fresh vegetables and 27 percent of the retail price of fresh fruits (Stewart 2006). Direct marketing can significantly increase the share of revenue kept by the farmer, while helping him or her to develop a loyal customer base.

That customer base is primarily in urban areas. Farmers' markets, Community Supported Agriculture, and sales directly to restaurants and institutions all offer farmers the opportunity to connect and develop ongoing relationships with urban customers and markets. Organizations like the Farmer-Chef Connection program, developed by Ecotrust's farm and foods program, aid farmers in developing relationships with restaurants and urban institutions such as schools and hospitals (Ecotrust 2008).

Inspired by the success of direct marketing of food products, local wood users and wood growers decided to adapt a local purchasing strategy to Oregon wood products. The Build Local Alliance, a Portland-based nonprofit, is connecting architects, engineers, and secondary wood-products manufacturers to local providers of responsibly grown wood. This organization conducts tours, holds events, and circulates information that helps suppliers and users of local sustainably grown wood products find each other (Build Local Alliance 2008). The common thread that connects these direct-marketing and buy-local strategies is that they are not arm's-length transactions; rather, they are *interactions and relationships* that require time to develop.

Urban-Rural Connections and Upgrading Clusters

Urban-rural connections are also important for improving the performance of the cluster. Many industries have begun to improve the speed and effectiveness of innovation and product development by integrating customers into the innovation process. This strategy fits well with the differentiation strategies of certification and direct marketing. A sophisticated local demand is one of the factors that contributes to competitive clusters (Porter 2000). Sophisticated, knowledgeable, quality-sensitive customers often offer clues to the direction of future demand in larger markets. Thus, they can assist industries in refining and adapting their products. Oregon's urban areas offer a sophisticated set of consumers for food and forest products. Oregon chefs, diners, builders, and architects are more likely to value high-quality food and forest products that are grown locally and sustainably. Thus they are leading trends in national and international markets. Integrating these consumers into the innovation process to compete globally requires creating stronger relationships between rural producers and urban consumers.

The craft-beer industry in Oregon offers an example of how quality-conscious Oregonians can lead a national trend and prepare local producers for a broader market. Oregon is the second-largest producer of hops in the United States, after Washington State (USDA 2008). Pacific Northwest hops are prized for the distinctive flavor they impart to a beer. The Oregon Brewers Guild and the Hop Commission work together to promote Oregon hops and Oregon beer. Portland, with more brewpubs than any other city in the United States, has a sophisticated base of beer drinkers that evaluate the beer and prepare the brewers to launch to a broader market.

Using Connections to Take the Next Steps

What are some next steps to improving relationships between urban and rural business and the economic outcomes for urban and rural enterprises? For the food and agriculture industry, it is important to focus on key trends in consumer demand and the implications for the value chain. For example, the trend toward more healthful eating presents a market opportunity among Oregon's health-conscious consumers. About 75 percent of adults in Oregon report not getting their recommended five servings of fruits and vegetables per day (Centers for Disease Control 2007). Oregon has a strong market concentration in fresh fruits and vegetables and, as we have discussed, Oregon producers have an opportunity to increase their profit margin by delivering more produce directly to consumers. Oregon farmers have an opportunity to continue to differentiate their products from those imported from California, Canada, and Mexico. The key advantage for them is the opportunity to develop and maintain a personal relationship with the buyer.

The current recession has sent demand for lumber to historic lows (Western Wood Products Association 2009). Yet buried in the bleak statistics is an opportunity to position Oregon wood products to capture demand as it rises when the recession eases. Canadian and other foreign lumber suppliers are losing market share to domestic producers. Oregon producers can use this pause in the market to strengthen their relationships with builders, architects, and manufacturers; to pursue certification; and to research new markets for Oregon forest products.

Clearly, these strategies require strong connections between rural farms and forests and urban links in the value chain. These connections must go beyond mere arm's-length transactions to become more like good marriages—relationships based on trust, honesty, integrity, and clear communication.

Bibliography

Allen, Jennifer H., and Thomas Potiowsky. 2008. "Portland's green building cluster: Economic trends and impacts." *Economic Development Quarterly* 22 (4), November: 303-15.

Applied Development Economics (ADE). 2006. *Oregon Food Processing Cluster Study*. June 15, 2006. Portland: Northwest Food Processors Association.

Build Local Alliance. 2008. http://www.buildlocalalliance.org. Accessed October 15, 2009.

Centers for Disease Control. 2007. *Behavioral Risk Factor Surveillance System* (CDC BRFSS 2007). Trends data. http://apps.nccd.cdc.gov/brfss/trends/. Accessed March 10, 2008.

Ecotrust. 2008. *The Farmer-Chef Connection*. http://www.ecotrust.org/foodfarms/farmerchef.html. Accessed October 15, 2008.

E. D. Hovee & Company. 2005. *Oregon Forest Cluster Analysis*. June. Portland: Oregon Forest Resources Institute.

Fletcher, Richard A., Paul W. Adams, and Steven R. Radosevich. 2002. *Comparison of Two Forest Certification Systems and Oregon Legal Requirements.* Final report to the Oregon Department of Forestry, Salem,. Corvallis: Forest Research Laboratory, Oregon State University.

Food Alliance. 2009. http://www.foodalliance.org/client-search/producers. Accessed October 15, 2009.

Ganguly, I., and I. L. Eastin. 2007. Material Substitution Trends in Residential Construction 1995, 1998, 2001 and 2004. CINTRAFOR Working Paper 108. Seattle: Center for International Trade in Forest Products, University of Washington.

Gibbs, Robert M., and Andrew Bernat, Jr. 1997. "Rural industry clusters raise local earnings." *Rural Development Perspectives*, USDA Economic Research Service, 12(3).

Granatstein, David, and Elizabeth Kirby. 2004. *Organic Farm Statistics 2004.* Center for Sustaining Agriculture and Natural Resources (CSANR). http://csanr.wsu.edu/Organic/OrganicStats.htm. Pullman: Washington State University. Accessed October 15, 2008.

Hammer, Roger. 2008. "Toward one Oregon? From (how) many Oregons? The demography of dichotomy." Paper presented at the symposium Toward One Oregon: Rural-Urban Interdependence, November 14, 2008, Salem.

Henry, Mark, and Mark Drabenstott. 1996. "A new micro view of the U.S. rural economy." *Economic Review* (2nd quarter 1996): 53-70.

Martin, Sheila A., Meg Merrick, Tia Henderson, Elizabeth Mylott, Kelly Haines, Colin Price, Amy Koski, and Becky Dann. 2008. *Planting Prosperity and Harvesting Health: Trade-Offs and Sustainability in the Oregon-Washington Food System.* Portland: Institute of Portland Metropolitan Studies, Portland State University.

Oregon Department of Agriculture. 2008. *Oregon Agripedia, 2007 Edition.* Table 10. http://oregon.gov/ODA/pub_agripedia.shtml#Statistics_section_online. Accessed October 15, 2008.

Oregon Employment Department. 2008. *Oregon Statewide 2007 Covered Employment and Wages.* 2007 summary report. www.qualityinfo.org. Accessed October 15, 2008.

Oregon Tilth. http://www.tilth.org/. Accessed July 24, 2009.

Parsons, James. 2009. *Supply Chain Relationships and Value Chain Design.* Report prepared for the New Zealand Nuffield Scholarship Trust. http://www.nuffield.org.nz/.

Porter, Michael. 1985. *Competitive Advantage: Creating and Sustaining Superior Performance.* New York: Free Press.

Porter, Michael. 2000. "Location, competition and economic development: Local clusters in a global economy." *Economic Development Quarterly* 14 (1): 15-34.

Porter, Michael, Christian Ketels, Kaia Miller, and Richard T. Brydan, 2004. *Competitiveness in Rural U.S. Regions: Learning and Research Agenda.* Boston: Institute for Strategy and Competitiveness, Harvard Business School.

Schmitz, Hubert. 2006 *Value Chain Analysis for Policy Makers and Practitioners.* Geneva: International Labour Office.

Stevens-Garmon, John, Chung L. Huang, and Biing-Hwan Lin. 2007. "Organic demand: a profile of consumers in the fresh produce market." *Choices* 22 (2): 109-15.

Stewart, Haden. 2006. *How Low Has the Farm Share of Retail Food Prices Really Fallen?* Economic Research Report Number 24, August 2006. Washington D.C.: Economic Research Service, U.S. Department of Agriculture.

U.S. Bureau of the Census. North American Industry Classification System. http://www.census.gov/eos/www/naics/. Accessed July 24, 2009.

U.S. Bureau of Economic Analysis. 2008. *Regional Economic Information System*. Table CA05. http://www.bea.gov/regional/reis/CA05fn.cfm. U.S. Department of Commerce, Washington, DC. Accessed October 15, 2008.

U.S. Department of Agriculture. 2007. *Census of Agriculture, Oregon State Profile*. http://www.agcensus.usda.gov/Publications/2007/Online_Highlights/County_Profiles/Oregon/index.asp. Washington, D.C. Accessed May 15, 2009.

U.S. Department of Agriculture. 2008. *National Hop Report*. December 2008. http://www.nass.usda.gov/Statistics_by_State/Washington/Publications/Hops/index.asp. Washington, D.C.: National Agricultural Statistics Service, U.S. Department of Agriculture.

U.S. Green Building Council. http://www.usgbc.org.

Western Wood Products Association. 2009. "Lumber markets expected to reach historic low before starting slow recovery in 2010." March 24, 2009. http://www2.wwpa.org/. Accessed October 1, 2009.

Williamson, Oliver E. 1981. "The economics of organization: The transaction cost approach." *American Journal of Sociology* 87 (3): 548-77.

Chapter 9
Reframing Our Common Cause in an Interdependent World

Ethan Seltzer
Michael Hibbard
Bruce Weber

The reality of interdependence between rural and urban Oregon is not difficult to grasp. Rural Oregonians travel to urban areas to shop and get specialized medical, educational, and legal/financial services, and they commute or move to cities for jobs. Urban Oregonians depend on rural places for food, water, energy, open space, and recreation.

It is not obvious, however, that there is a strong case for rural and urban areas working together for a better common future. There is indeed a long history of urban-rural competition and conflict (Chapters 3 and 4). There is evidence of a weakening of economic ties between Portland-Vancouver and the surrounding economic region (Chapter 5) and of increasing transfers of public funds from the Portland metropolitan area to the rest of the state (Chapter 6). And one important economic cluster that appeared to have promise for both rural and urban Oregon—the wood-products sector (Chapter 8) —has seen precipitous declines in the past several decades.

Furthermore, most of the current intellectual excitement about economic growth focuses on the vitality of urban centers and the beneficial effects of urban growth on the surrounding regional economy. Much of this excitement draws on modern economic insights from "new growth theory" and "new economic geography" about the central and critical roles of new knowledge and technology, knowledge spillovers, and increasing returns in economic growth. Simply put, it is argued that cities create the conditions for people and ideas to interact, and it is this interaction that lies at the heart of economic innovation and progress.

However, this literature often acknowledges the importance of larger forces that affect the economic fortunes of both cities and rural places: economic restructuring, globalization, and policy decisions made far from the borders of any particular city region. The dominant thrust of this literature is that the drivers of economic progress are the ideas generated in the urban knowledge hubs to which the creative class is drawn and where increasing returns make implementation of these ideas profitable. Because of their remoteness from urban hubs, rural areas cannot as easily participate in the exchanges and dynamics underlying this new global economy.

Even though cities are the engines of growth, it is not just cities that benefit from urban vitality. Workers in the surrounding countryside commute to the cities and bring their earnings back home, and businesses set up operations in the surrounding countryside (where land, labor, and housing costs are often lower) to produce goods and services to sell to businesses in the nearby cities. These "spillovers" of urban growth can extend far into the hinterland but are generally stronger in places closest to the cities because of greater ease of access. Proximity to urban shopping and recreational and cultural amenities make rural areas near cities more attractive than remote rural areas to many workers and their families.

Many scholars have shown that rural areas benefit from proximity to a healthy urban core. In a study of U.S. counties, Wu and Gopinath (2008) found that "remoteness is a primary cause of spatial disparities in economic development" (392). Henry et al. (1997) found in a study of the southeastern United States that urban growth spreads to rural and exurban areas, generating new transactions and economic forces. Partridge et al. (2007), in their study of income and population growth in Canada, concluded that growth spreads up to about one hundred miles into rural areas. In a study of rural job growth in the United States, Partridge et al. (2008) found that proximity to urban areas was one of the strongest predictors of rural job growth. Partridge and Clark (2008) conclude from this literature that, far outside the cities, income earned from urban jobs helps support other jobs in rural and exurban communities, such as those in local retail establishments or rural businesses. Urban-based jobs help maintain a viable rural and exurban population base that facilitates community vitality (20). Feser and Isserman (2006), in their examination of urban spatial spillovers in the United States, found "evidence of net positive spread of employment growth spillovers from proximate urban counties ('spread effects')" (26).

However, the city-centric new economic geography and the extensive urban-spillover literature tend not to focus on either the extent to which rural places have sources of economic vitality that do not depend on proximity to a city, or the impact of state, national, and global forces on rural places. Nor do they often consider the fact that growth or decline in this autonomous rural economy has spillover effects, positive and negative, on the urban core that are often relatively larger than the impacts of urban trade on the rural economy (Chapter 5).

The benign neglect of the rural periphery leaves the impression that larger national and global forces tend to influence the rural areas through their impact on cities. Indeed, it is a source of rural discontent that state and national policymakers often fail to recognize that their policy decisions have an independent and differential effect on rural places, an effect that does not work its way through urban centers. Thinking specifically about Oregon, it is possible, without falling into either urban fundamentalism or rural/agricultural/natural-resource fundamentalism, to articulate both the economic activity that is interdependent and that which is independent for both the Portland metropolitan area core and the rural periphery. Clarifying these factors would likely facilitate the identification of new opportunities for mutually beneficial interaction, and it would reveal the extent to which national and global forces differentially affect Portland and the rest of the state.

Cortright (2009) examined the promising prospects for the Portland metro regional economy and concluded that one important dimension of regional competitive advantage is "distinctiveness." Cortright argues that an important component of Portland's distinctiveness is its long-standing culture of sustainability, which positions it well for leadership in green industries. Portland's reputation for concern about sustainability (and an associated "foodie" culture that values local food, wine, brewpubs, and coffeehouses) evolved in the unique geographic context of the northern Willamette Valley and depends to some extent on a vital rural periphery.

Another important asset noted by Cortright is the concentrations of local talent. The distinctiveness of Portland's food, drink, outdoors-recreation-loving, and green-environmental-sustainability culture may also have made the metro area particularly attractive to young, highly educated workers. During the previous decade, Cortright asserts, Portland has attracted young college graduates at a rate five times greater than the national growth rate of this population.

Portland's distinctiveness and competitive advantage, then, rest to an important extent on its location in a spectacular setting, framed by mountains, characterized by abundance, and with ready access to wilderness, ocean beaches, and a vital working landscape. Further, if the extent of Portland's embeddedness in its rural periphery is unique among the nation's cities, then Portland's competitiveness depends on the health of its surrounding rural areas to a greater extent than is true for other U.S. cities. Certainly the case can be made that the distinctiveness of Portland would be seriously weakened if Oregon's rural communities, landscapes, and natural resources were to degrade and atrophy.

There are strong voices exhorting cities and suburbs to work together (Greenstein and Wievel 2000). Few, though, take a broader look across the whole urban-rural continuum. Partridge and Clark (2008) examine Ohio's "geography of urban and rural interdependencies," but their focus is primarily on the extensive commuting between exurban and suburban counties and the urban core economies. In part this is because in Ohio, in contrast to Oregon, "virtually the entire state's population lives within a one-hour drive of an urbanized area [of fifty thousand or more population] and are reliant on the associated jobs, services and recreational venues—as well as the associated economic spillovers from these cities" (2). Dabson (2007) is one of very few voices to emphasize both the rural contributions to urban places and the urban contributions to rural places.

In this book we have tried to establish the foundation for a statewide conversation about Oregon and the future of the diverse communities along the urban-rural continuum. The reality is that Oregon is not a simple urban core surrounded by a rural periphery. It is a variegated quilt of densely and sparsely populated places, some growing and some not, distributed not quite randomly across a resource-rich natural landscape. These places are interconnected within a loosely defined, ever-changing hierarchy of larger and smaller population centers.

Where do we go from here? What does this mean for Oregon? We believe that, knowingly or not, Oregon faces a choice. Will we deliberately seek a strategic approach to knitting together the parts of Oregon into a whole? Or will we take the path of least resistance and continue to approach the future of Oregon as a win-lose proposition between the varied regions and interests that make up the state? The latter is familiar; we know that route. But as the chapters presented here illustrate, continuing on that route will not produce the strategic thinking that is essential to allow Oregon to compete effectively in a global economy and in national policy discussions.

We have tried to demonstrate that globalization has had a profound impact on our politics and economy. It has created both opportunities—as witnessed by the migration of talented, educated people to Oregon—as well as challenges to our ability to sustain both rural and urban quality of life. We need to accept that the challenges faced by rural Oregon are not due to something done by urban Oregon, and the challenges faced by urban Oregon are not due to something done by rural Oregon.

We know from work presented in this book that "core" and "periphery" in Oregon are not as tightly linked economically as they once were. As is the case throughout the world, economic relationships are not solely determined by state-level institutions, if they ever were. Though public policy has had and will have a profound impact on markets, livability, and trade, its promulgation at the state level plays an essential though limited role in a global economy. However, as has long been the case, the periphery depends on the core and the core depends on the periphery, although not in the same ways as in the past.

Whereas once Portland was the sole gateway to the world for the products of the periphery, this is no longer the case. Whereas the economic prospects of those in the core were once intimately tied to the productive capacity of the land, those prospects are now linked to new endeavors, most of which have more to do with technology and global clusters than with climate and soil. These trends are in motion and are unlikely to be turned around. Old links are weaker, and new relationships, though maybe not as strong, nonetheless will form the basis for what comes next. The Oregon "core" and "periphery" are not likely to find common ground based on historical relationships. We need something new and probably more limited on which to focus our collective effort and collective future.

Consequently, we need to reframe our common cause. We need to think about what we can do together to become more competitive in a global economy. What does the world want, and what can we, urban and rural, provide? Witness the action by Tektronix early in the twenty-first century to spurn the advances of both Oregon and Washington in favor of the bright lights and cheaper labor costs of Shanghai. Bigger roads and deeper ports are not the missing links or the solution. We need twenty-first-century strategies for global competitiveness, and we need to learn quickly how to sort out the nineteenth-century claims dominating state-level policy discussions.

That said, we need to pick and choose carefully from our past. The challenge is not to forget or forsake the past and its legacy, but to understand better what aspects of that legacy will propel us into the future. In addition to focusing outward, we also need to deepen the discussion internally by building community. For example, we know that Oregonians have deep affinity for the landscape and natural environment we share. Survey research sponsored by the Oregon Business Council and others has demonstrated a high degree of common commitment to core values from both urban and rural communities (Oregon Values and Beliefs 2002).

We introduced this book with the assertion that Oregonians share many aspirations and hopes. It is our hope that, as we discuss Oregon's future, we can focus on issues that urban and rural people agree are key to productive and healthy lives and communities—education, health care, transportation—and on issues that are critical to the success of "leading" industries such as food, nature, and sustainability, that build on the distinctive relationship between the Portland metropolitan area and the rest of the state.

There is no one among us who doesn't recognize the extraordinary beauty of the Oregon landscape, wherever we live, and the promise that it provides. However, we often disagree on how to care for it. We need to focus less on means and more on ends, and in that way create a broader constituency for the state as a place, as a whole.

Finally, we need to agree, at least in the near term, to shorten the list of issues that we're attempting to manage. We need to focus government at the state level on services that lead to global competitiveness, and to agree to check other issues and agendas at the door. We need to focus on the things that unite us, and to agree to disagree on the things that don't. In time, perhaps, we can address it all, but for now we need to pick and choose carefully, in a way that helps us relearn how to engage the world as one.

Our hope is that this book will help us all to see Oregon in a new light. We can use what we've learned, or we can ignore it. It is very exciting and promising to know that we can make our interdependencies in Oregon the basis for stronger and more strategic relationships among our communities. It is equally daunting to consider the thoughtfulness, commitment, and perseverance this will require.

Bibliography

Cortright, Joe. 2009. "The City University Partnership: Applying the *City Vitals* Framework to Creating a Sustainable Region." Draft white paper submitted to "Building University-Community Partnerships for a Sustainable Regional Economy, Portland State University."

Dabson, Brian. 2007. "Rural-urban interdependence: Why metropolitan and rural America need each other." Background paper prepared for the Blueprint for American Prosperity. The Brookings Institution, Washington, D.C. http://www.brookings.edu/projects/blueprint.aspx.

Feser, Edward, and Andrew M. Isserman. 2006. *Harnessing Growth Spillovers for Rural Development: The Effects of Regional Spatial Structure.* Urbana-Champaign, Ill.: Report to USDA Rural Development.

Greenstein, Rosalind, and Wim Wievel, eds. 2000. *Urban-Suburban Interdependencies.* Cambridge Mass.: Lincoln Institute of Land Policy.

Henry, M. S., D. L. Barkley, and S. Bao. 1997. "The hinterland's stake in metropolitan area growth." *Journal of Regional Science* 37(3):479-501.

Oregon Values and Beliefs. 2002. Survey sponsored by Oregon Business Council, Oregon Education Association, Oregon School Boards Association, and SIEU Local 503 of the Oregon Public Employees Union. http://www.oregonvalues.org/. Accessed September 21, 2009.

Partridge, Mark D., Ray Bollman, M. Rose Olfert, and Alessandro Alasia. 2007. "Riding the wave of urban growth in the countryside: spread, backwash, or stagnation." *Land Economics* 83(2): 128-52.

Partridge, Mark D., Dan S. Rickman, Kamar Ali, and M. Rose Olfert. 2008. "Employment growth in the American urban hierarchy: long live distance." *B. E. Journal of Macroeconomics.* 8(1) (Contributions), Article 10. http://www.bepress.com/bejm/vol8/iss1/art10. Accessed March 13, 2008.

Partridge, Mark D., and Jill Clark. 2008. *Our Joint Future: Rural-Urban Interdependence in 21st Century Ohio.* Draft white paper prepared for the Brookings Institution, Washington D.C.

Wu, JunJie, and Munisamy Gopinath. 2008. "What causes spatial variations in economic development in the United States?" *American Journal of Agricultural Economics* 90(2): 392-408.

Notes

Preface

[1] Toward One Oregon: Rural-Urban Interdependence. November 14, 2008. Salem Convention Center, Salem.

Chapter Two

[1] We gratefully acknowledge the research assistance of Emily Picha and Becky Dann.

[2] When the metropolitan areas were defined by the U.S. Bureau of the Budget for the 1950 census, there were three metropolitan counties in Oregon: Multnomah, Clackamas, and Washington. These three plus Clark County, Washington State, constituted the Portland-Vancouver Standard Metropolitan Statistical Area (SMSA). Lane County was added as the Eugene SMSA in 1960 by the U.S. Office of Management and Budget. In 1971, the Salem SMSA, composed of Marion and Polk counties, was defined. In 1973, the Eugene-Springfield SMSA was defined as Lane County. Jackson County was added as the Medford SMSA in 1981. Yamhill County was added to the Portland-Vancouver SMSA in 1983, and Columbia County was added in 1993. In 1999, the Corvallis SMSA was defined as Benton County. In 2003, Skamania County, Washington, was added to the Portland-Vancouver SMSA and the Bend SMSA was defined as Deschutes County. See U.S. Census Bureau, *Metropolitan and Micropolitan Statistical Areas*.

[3] "Places" are defined by the U.S. Census Bureau as "a concentration of population either legally bounded as an incorporated place or delineated for statistical purposes as a census-designated place." By this definition, a place includes cities, towns, villages, and other incorporated areas, as well as some unincorporated areas that are identifiable by name and recognized by the Census Bureau for the purpose of presenting census data. See Isserman (2005) for a concise and insightful discussion of the complexities involved in defining urban and rural.

[4] Medically underserved areas (MUA) and medically underserved populations (MUP) are defined by the Health Resources and Services Administration of the U.S. Department of Health and Human Services, http://bhpr.hrsa.gov/shortage/muaguide.htm. Oregon's MUA/MUP map is available at http://www.flu.oregon.gov/DHS/ph/hsp/hpshortage/muap.pdf.

Chapter Three

[1] In 1900, Portland led Seattle by 90,426 to 80,871. In 1910 Seattle led with 237,174 residents to Portland's 207,214.

[2] See the maps of paved roads for 1910, 1920, and 1930 in Loy et al. (2001).

[3] Support for the Klan among a broadly defined middle class is described in Jackson 1967, Chalmers 1987, and Moore 1991.

[4] In 2008 the Census Bureau defined a seven-county Portland metropolitan area that includes Clark and Skamania counties in Washington and Multnomah, Washington, Clackamas, Columbia, and Yamhill counties in Oregon. Measurement is also complicated by the fact that in the 1990s the census designated Portland and Salem as a Consolidated Metropolitan Statistical Area, but has removed that designation in recent years. This chapter omits Washington State's population, using the three core counties for 1940-1980 and the larger five-county area for the most recent decade.

[5] See maps of freight corridors in Loy et al. 2001.

[6] On the coast, the prison at Tillamook was expanded and a new facility was built at North Bend. East of the Cascades, the prison at Pendleton was expanded and new prisons were built at Ontario, Baker City, Umatilla, Lakeview, and Madras. The federal prison at Sheridan just sneaks into the metropolitan category.

[7] It failed in Wallowa County by twenty-three votes, in Morrow County by eighty-four votes, and in Baker County by 181 votes.

Chapter Four

[1] My most detailed effort to develop this argument is in *Colony and Empire: The Capitalist Transformation of the American West* (Robbins 1994).

[2] For a further elaboration of this argument, see Stavrianos 1976, 168-69.

[3] Ann Markusen (1987, 4) points out that conflict arises when owners of transportation and finance live in one area and producers live in another.

[4] These ideas reflect the arguments of Berend and Ranki 1982 and McCormick 1990.

[5] I use the term "resettlement" to refer to the displacement of Native people from valuable agricultural and other lands to more marginal places in much of the West.

[6] For general studies that address these themes, see Harvey 1985, Trachtenberg 1982, and Agnew 1987.

[7] See also Jeff Moore's account at http://www.trainweb.org/highdesertrails/oprr.html.

[8] For the origins of the conflict in the Umpqua Valley, see Robbins 1969, 90-92, and the Roseburg *Plaindealer* 1873.

[9] Because it operated "cash-only cooperatives," Lawrence Goodwyn contends, the Grange "failed to address the real ills of farmers," who lacked the cash to participate in such ventures (Goodwyn 1978, 32).

[10] Two books that shaped my thinking for this section of the essay are Johnston 2003 and Lipin 2007.

[11] For the immediate postwar boom, see Robbins 2004, 21-46.

[12] The rural-urban wage gap has widened during the past thirty years. Some of the increase is attributable to declining timber harvests, but much is related to the growing high-tech sector along the Interstate 5 corridor. See the Salem *Statesman-Journal,* Aug. 30, 2008.

Chapter Five

[1] The BEA has changed the definitions and boundaries of the economic areas many times since first defining them in 1969; the most recent changes were in 2004. We use the early 1980s BEA definition and boundaries throughout this chapter so that both our analyses (1982 and 2006) may deal with the same core and periphery areas.

[2] That is, of what IMPLAN calls "gross commodity supply."

[3] In core-periphery economic analysis, a spillover effect is a measure of the effect of economic activity in one subregion on the economy of the other, expressed as a coefficient. For example, a periphery-to-core spillover coefficient of 0.17 for the 1982 livestock sector indicates that the core economy gets $0.17 of every dollar of total impact associated with increase in livestock-sector exports from the periphery. See table 7 in the Appendix for spillover coefficients for the Portland trade area.

[4] Indirect impacts are those related to local respending by local businesses of money received supplying inputs to the exporting industry. Induced impacts are those related to local respending by households of income earned in the production of these goods and services.

Chapter Six

[1] With research assistance from Mersiha Spahic, Portland State University.

Chapter Seven

[1] Inglehart's short version of the postmaterialist indicator was used in the survey. The survey question asks: "There is a lot of talk these days about what our country's goals should be for the next ten or fifteen years. Listed below are some goals that different people say should be given top priority. Please mark the one you consider the most important in the long run. What would be your second choice? Please mark that second choice as well. Possible choices include: (1) Maintaining order in the nation; (2) Fighting rising prices; (3) Giving people more say in important governmental decisions; (4) Protecting freedom of speech." Respondents selecting (1) and (2) are coded as "materialist," while those selecting (3) and (4) are "postmaterialist." Remaining options are considered "mixed" values. See Inglehart 1977, 1990, 1997.

[2] The survey of Oregon city-government officials was conducted by Oregon State University, the University of Oregon, and the League of Oregon Cities during fall 2005 and winter 2006.

[3] This area encompasses the counties of Baker, Crook, Deschutes, Gilliam, Grant, Harney, Hood River, Jefferson, Klamath, Lake, Malheur, Morrow, Sherman, Umatilla, Union, Wallowa, Wasco, and Wheeler.

[4] The western Oregon counties of Coos, Curry, Douglas, Jackson, and Josephine.

[5] Linn, Marion, Polk, and Yamhill counties.

[6] For a discussion of the importance of tourism to these four counties, see Knoder 2005.

[7] For example, see the analysis by Mapes (2006) regarding the decline of Republican control over the suburbs as the party became more culturally conservative and less business oriented.

[8] By September 2010, Democratic Party registration had dropped one percentage point overall in the eastern, southern, and university counties from the 2008 figures shown in table 6. There was no change in the other regions (Oregon Secretary of State 2010b).

Contributors

CARL ABBOTT is professor of urban studies and planning at Portland State University, where he has taught since 1978. He holds degrees in history from Swarthmore College and the University of Chicago. His central interest is in the ways in which the growth of North American cities has shaped and interacted with the continent's economic and cultural regions. His books on this topic include *Political Terrain: Washington, D.C. from Tidewater Town to Global Metropolis* (1999), *Greater Portland: Urban Life and Landscape in the Pacific Northwest* (2001), and *How Cities Won the West: Four Centuries of Urban Change in Western North America* (2008). He is also interested in the ways in which literature and popular culture respond to American regions, which is the subject of his book *Frontiers Past and Future: Science Fiction and the American West* (2006).

RICHARD A. CLUCAS is professor of political science in the Mark Hatfield School of Government at Portland State University and executive director of the Western Political Science Association, the nation's second-largest regional political science association. Clucas received his bachelor's degree from the University of California at Irvine and his master's and doctorate from the University of California at Santa Barbara. His research focuses on legislative politics, state government, and Oregon politics. Among other works, he is editor of *Readings and Cases in State and Local Politics* and co-editor of *Oregon Politics and Government: Progressives versus Conservative Populists*. He is also the series editor of *About U.S. State Government: An Encyclopedia of the Executive, Legislative, and Judicial Branches*. He is particularly interested in how rural-urban dynamics influence legislative policy making.

JOSEPH CORTRIGHT is president of Impresa, Inc., a Portland economic consulting firm. He holds a bachelor's degree from Lewis and Clark College and a master's in public policy from the University of California at Berkeley.

171

He is a non-resident Senior Fellow at the Brookings Institution and a senior research advisor for CEOs for Cities, a national organization of urban leaders based in Chicago. He currently serves as the chair of the Oregon Governor's Council of Economic Advisers. For three decades Cortright has been actively involved in economic development policy making in Oregon.

BETH EMSHOFF is director of Oregon Open Campus for Oregon State University and a faculty member with the OSU Extension Service in Portland. She received her bachelor's and master's degrees from the University of Wisconsin at Madison and studied educational leadership at the University of St. Thomas. She joined the OSU faculty after twenty-five years at the University of Minnesota, where she was a research fellow, senior administrator for outreach and engagement programs in human ecology, and Extension associate dean and program leader. Her task in Oregon is to reinvent Extension's role in the Portland metropolitan area to meet the needs of urban residents. To that end she has integrated metropolitan issues and perspectives into OSU Extension programs and planning, facilitated partnerships with Portland State University, where she has her office, developed a model for urban Extension, and provided the leadership for the Toward One Oregon symposium and book project.

MARK HENKELS is professor of political science/public policy and administration at Western Oregon University in Monmouth. He received his bachelor's in history from Whitman College, his master's in foreign affairs from the University of Virginia, and his doctorate in political science from the University of Utah. Henkels's career at WOU centers around public policy with particular emphasis on state government, aging, and administrative law. His current research concerns Oregon state politics and the policy challenges posed by our aging society. His long-standing interest in the rural-urban divide in Oregon is reinforced by living on a very small farm between Corvallis and Albany.

MICHAEL HIBBARD is director of the Institute for Policy Research and Innovation and professor of planning, public policy and management at the University of Oregon. He is a participating faculty member in the Environmental Studies, Historic Preservation, and International Studies programs at the University of Oregon and a faculty affiliate in the Oregon State

University Rural Studies Program. He received his doctorate in regional planning from the University of California at Los Angeles. His work focuses on community and regional development, with a special emphasis on the social impacts of regional economic change in the United States and internationally. He has published widely on rural socioeconomic development, conservation-based development, and indigenous community planning. Before entering the academic world he worked for more than ten years in planning and community development.

DAVID HOLLAND is professor emeritus in the School of Economic Sciences at Washington State University in Pullman. He received his bachelor's and master's degrees from Colorado State University and his doctorate from Oklahoma State. His fields of interest include regional economics and modeling systems pertaining to agricultural development and regional economics. He has twice been a visiting professor at the University of Chile in Santiago, teaching economic modeling. His teaching specialties are operations research, economic impact analysis, and growth and change in the West. Research specialties are general equilibrium analysis, economic evaluation, and input-output analysis. He has considerable international experience as an agricultural economist in Kenya and Lesotho and is fluent in Spanish.

PAUL LEWIN is a graduate research assistant in the Department of Agricultural and Resource Economics at Oregon State University. He received his bachelor's and master's degrees from the Pontifical Catholic University of Chile. He conducts research on the causes and consequences of food insecurity and rural poverty, determinants and impacts of rural-urban migration, and urban-rural economic interdependence. He has worked with public-expenditure and food-security policy for the United Nations Food and Agriculture Organization (FAO) at its regional office in Santiago, Chile, and at its Rome headquarters. He has also worked as a researcher and instructor at the Catholic University of Chile.

SHEILA MARTIN is director of the Institute of Portland Metropolitan Studies, a service and research institute in the School of Urban Studies and Planning at Portland State University. She received her bachelor's degree from Southern Illinois University, her master's from the University of Kentucky, and her doctorate from Iowa State University. Prior to joining PSU in 2004,

Martin served as economic development advisor to Washington Governor Gary Locke. Before that she was a senior economist at the Research Triangle Institute, North Carolina, where she built a research program in technology, economics, and policy and conducted research on the value of innovation and the impact of technology in industry.

WILLIAM G. ROBBINS is distinguished professor of history emeritus at Oregon State University. He received a bachelor's degree from Western Connecticut University in 1962 and then migrated west, earning his doctorate in history at the University of Oregon in 1969. He taught at Western Oregon University before joining the Oregon State University faculty in 1971, where he taught courses in Pacific Northwest history, history of the American West, and environmental history. Robbins has authored and edited eleven books, most recently *Landscapes of Conflict: The Oregon Story, 1940-2000* (2004), *Oregon, This Storied Land* (2005), and, with coauthor Katrine Barber, *Nature's Northwest: The North Pacific Slope in the Twentieth Century* (2011).

ETHAN SELTZER is a professor in the Nohad A. Toulan School of Urban Studies and Planning at Portland State University. He previously served for six years as the director of the school, and before that was the founding director of PSU's Institute of Portland Metropolitan Studies. He received his bachelor's degree from Swarthmore College, his master's in regional planning from the University of Pennsylvania, and his doctorate in city and regional planning, also from Penn. Before joining PSU in 1992 Seltzer served as land-use supervisor for Metro, the regional government in the Portland area; as assistant to Portland city commissioner Mike Lindberg; as assistant coordinator for the Southeast Uplift Neighborhood Program in Portland; and as drinking-water project coordinator for the Oregon Environmental Council. Current research interests are regional planning, regionalism, regional development, and planning in the Pacific Northwest. Related publications include "Maintaining the Working Landscape: The Portland Metro Urban Growth Boundary" in *Regional Planning for Open Space* (2009) and "It's Not an Experiment: Regional Planning at Metro, 1990 to the Present" in *The Portland Edge* (2004).

BRUCE SORTE is community economist in the Department of Agricultural and Resource Economics at Oregon State University. He received his bachelor's and master's degrees at Oregon State University. He teaches microeconomics and analyzes the economic impacts of policy options for state and local government agencies and organizations on topics as varied as globalization, critical habitat for fish, child care, viability of small farms, and grazing on public lands. In his outreach activities, he travels around Oregon east of the Cascades towing his 1968 Airstream trailer, helping local communities increase their economic resilience with programs focusing on business retention, expansion, and improved competitiveness. He has published numerous Extension Special Reports that can be found on the OSU Rural Studies Program website.

BRENT S. STEEL is professor of political science at Oregon State University and director of the university's Master of Public Policy program. He received his bachelor's degree in government from Eastern Washington University and his master's and doctorate in political science from Washington State University. Steel is coeditor, with Richard A. Clucas and Mark Henkels, of *Oregon Politics and Government: Progressives versus Conservative Populists* and coauthor, with Chris Simon and Nicholas P. Lovrich, of *State and Local Government: Sustainability in the 21st Century*.

BRUCE WEBER is director of the Rural Studies Program and professor of agricultural and resource economics, Oregon State University. He received his bachelor's degree from Seattle University and his master's and doctorate from the University of Wisconsin at Madison. His research focuses on the causes of poverty and hunger in rural areas, particularly on how community characteristics and public policy influence economic outcomes for low-income people. He provides leadership to Extension programs that deal with rural policy, economic and social conditions in rural communities, and the interplay of poverty, hunger, and antipoverty programs in rural America.

Index

Made in the USA
Coppell, TX
13 September 2021